MW00800303

About the Author

A trailblazer of Persian cookery. Rebekah Jones was born in Coventry to a Persian father and an English mother. Rebekah lives in North Shropshire with her husband Darren and her little boy, Kasper. A self-taught cook and a Persian food enthusiast, Rebekah has a passion for bringing Persian and Middle Eastern food into people's homes while showing just how accessible and delicious it is.

Rebekah is the host of regular successful Shropshire Supper Clubs and Pop Ups and she is the writer of the 'My Little Persian Kitchen' blog.

My Little Persian Kitchen is her first book.

Connect with Rebekah at
https://mylittlepersiankitchen.com/contact/

MY LITTLE PERSIAN KITCHEN

Rebekah Jones

MY LITTLE PERSIAN KITCHEN

Recipes Inspired by Persia
From my table to yours

Vanguard Press

VANGUARD PAPERBACK

© Copyright 2020
Rebekah Jones

A CIP catalogue record for this title is
available from the British Library.

ISBN 978 1 78465 675 1

*Vanguard Press is an imprint of
Pegasus Elliot MacKenzie Publishers Ltd.*
www.pegasuspublishers.com

First Published in 2020

**Vanguard Press
Sheraton House Castle Park
Cambridge England**

Printed & Bound in Great Britain

Dedication

For my darling son, Kasper, who is my reason for being. He has helped me bake, cook and he has tried all the recipes in this book and most importantly, he has taken the tradition of licking the spoon over from his mummy.

Acknowledgements

I would like to thank a handful of wonderful people who I am lucky enough to have been surrounded by.

To the team at Pegasus Publishing, for helping to bring my dream to life and for always answering my constant questions and being so patient with me throughout my many, many, amends and requests.

To Rob and Lynne and the wonderful team at Alderford Lake who let me take over their beautiful setting time and time again, to run my supper clubs.

To Hayley and Jess for giving up your time to come and have a 'night out' and work for me, wait tables, wash up and wipe away my tears and of course take photos at my supper clubs.

To my dad and my mum, who showed me the kind of person that I wanted to be and to never give up!

To Claire, my lovely friend, grammar queen, head waitress, photographer, cake eater, the first and only person to ever call me a rock star.

To my wonderful best friend, Rachel, who loves me unconditionally and is my biggest truth speaker!

To my mother-in-law, Diane, who always tells me that I can do anything and how proud of me she is.

To my Aunty Ane-Marie, who spent hours and hours with me as a young girl, teaching me to bake. She always let me put the weights on the scales and lick the spoon!

To my Uncle Ali'gator', who is always sourcing ingredients for me to use and telling me how proud he is of me.

To my amazing stepson, Isaac, for creating the term 'scratchy rice' and for eating so much of it!

To my beautiful son, Kasper. I love you to the moon and back a zillion times.

And finally, to my husband, Darren who loves to eat my food and nourishes my soul. This, after all, was his idea in the first place! Thank you for your endless support, advice and ideas, for loving me even when I am shouting about spilt milk and for always tasting my food!

Contents

Introduction

Imagine being a nine-year-old little girl telling your grandmother, who had flown over from Iran and who now stood cooking in your aunt's kitchen, 'You are doing that wrong!'

Well that was me then, telling my grandmother who had cooked daily for years that she was doing it wrong! And I do that now, I make notes on every single recipe that I try out of a book and I make tweaks and changes to flavours and seasoning and cooking times. I am a self-confessed recipe busy body! Every page in every book I own (and there are many) is battered, stained from spilt ingredients and crinkled. I love that. After all, isn't it a books purpose to be loved, read, and used over and over again?

I have always had a serious case of wanderlust. Nothing pleases me more than exploring new countries and new cultures.

I think it stems from growing up in the UK as an Iranian girl in a majority British village where no one knew that a country called Iran existed.

As a small child, I used to wonder where my family heritage came from and if Iran was really a place. It may sound bizarre but I didn't know.

Iran wasn't part of any history curriculum while I was at school, yet most of us now know the history of the Persian empire and of Alexander the Great's conquest.

In today's society, Iran is shrouded in political opinion and it evokes fear and uncertainty in people. Yet Iran through the eyes of my family is quite a different place, not too far a cry from people's perception of Persia. More like 'cream cakes and rose gardens' than 'rice and desert land!'

My dad and my uncle tell me stories of the bazaars, the mountains that they used to ski on, the seas, the sweet cream cakes as big as your hands and the kebab as juicy and delicious as anything that you have ever tried.

Before we had our little one, my husband and I spent all our spare pennies on travel and music. If we weren't visiting a new European city in any given month we were going to a gig, a concert or a festival.

The thing that I love about visiting new places is not sitting in a five-star resort, enjoying being waited on hand and foot (my hubbie disagrees), but soaking up the culture, hearing the noise of the country, seeing the colours and tasting the food.

Food is so intrinsic to a country's culture, and it is never far from religion. It inspires. It nourishes. It makes you smile from within.

My cooking and most of the food which you will find adorned on these pages is influenced by my travels, my childhood and by my Aunty Ane-Marie and my Uncle Ali who used to cook for me when I stayed with them during the Summer; food from my childhood that my Mother and my Father cooked for us and some recipes and stories along the way of the years gone by and the places I have visited and have eaten in. You learn so much about a country from its food and I for one, would happily plot my trips based on the food and the culture of a new place, over a hotel star rating any day.

My favourite recipes in this book are, 'Ghormeh Sabzi' as it holds so many lovely memories for me and the smell of it cooking is indescribable and 'Sholeh-zard,' because this was always my birthday treat as a little girl and whenever I eat it now, I still feel like my daddy's little princess!

My aunt used to say that whenever I baked as a little girl, I used to pose for a photo holding my treats with a grin on my face that stretched from ear to ear ... I still have that same grin when I open the oven and I find something that I have lovingly cooked inside.

I absolutely adore cooking for my friends, and for my family. I love to share my food, recipes and any tips I have learnt along the way, which is why I initially set up my blog. I love to share recipes that I have found and loved; family recipes that have been passed down and recipes that I have created myself, with as many people as I can possibly reach. So, here my adventure continues, and I hope that it will be a long one.

Store cupboard essentials

One of the things that I find utterly amazing about Persian cooking and cooking in general is how a collection of ingredients can take on a totally different identity when they come together with other ingredients, to form a dish, a cake or a treat. Never has the phrase 'The whole is greater than the sum of its parts' applied more than when discussing food.

One of the main things that I have been asked over the years when we have friends over for dinner is where do I source my ingredients from? And what should people have in stock if they want to be able to cook Persian food?

So here it is, a quick store cupboard essentials list of non-perishable items that you will find in most of my recipes.

Rose - you can read more about the use of rose on my blog 'the gift of a rose'. However, as a quick overview, Rosewater is great to add to khoreshts (Persian stews), stews and cakes if you want the flavour notes to run throughout a dish. Use the dried petals as a pretty garnish, or steep in tea.

Turmeric - this lovely yellow powder is great if used properly. My dad taught me to always fry off the turmeric with onions before adding any meat to a dish as this takes the bitterness out of it and gives it a deeper flavour and colour.

Cardamom - both ground and pods. Green cardamom for adding an aromatic flavour to sweet or savoury dishes. Black cardamom if you are opting to add a coolness like mint to a dish.

Omani limes - you can buy these little dried limes online or from a good Asian or Middle Eastern food store. You can also buy them ground in powder form. I love them whole added to my stews and tagines and I pierce them just before throwing them in so that they don't burst during cooking.

Saffron - my favourite of all the spices. These little red strands are the most expensive spice in the world by weight and the best saffron in the world comes from Iran. The reason for this is the richness of the soil in Iran. Although the country has little rainfall there is a system of underground aqueducts called qanats. These aqueducts supply water to over seventy percent of the country's farms and households. You can buy Iranian saffron online. However if you cannot buy it online then supermarket saffron will do. Just make sure that you grind it with sugar and dissolve it in rosewater or warm water before adding it to your dish.

Cumin - seeds and ground. If you are using the seeds always toast them first to bring out the flavour.

Advieh - you can make your own advieh if you are feeling adventurous or you can purchase it from a Middle Eastern food market. It is a household spice combination in the same way as 'Garam Masala' or 'Ras el hanout'. I use this in rice and tagines or in khoreshts.

Tinned tomatoes - there is nothing wrong with using tinned tomatoes instead of fresh and don't be afraid to use passata as an alternative if you wish. I always keep around 5 or 6 tins in my cupboard just in case I feel like an impromptu khoresht (which happens more often than you would think).

Basmati rice - My dad and my uncle always buy my rice for me. They buy me a 20kg sack and this normally lasts until I get another visit from either of them. I'm not suggesting that you rush out and buy a 20kg sack. However, with rice I would recommend getting a good strong Basmati not a cheap version as it makes a lot of difference to the length and the strength of the grain. You can tell a good basmati as the grains stay long and firm when cooked and they don't break in half easily. Always wash the rice until the water runs clear before cooking. This removes excess starch and any impurities in the rice and also prevents sticking and clumping.

Sabzi - You can put a bowl of 'sabzi' (Persian fresh chopped herbs) to accompany a meal. For some khoreshts you can use dried herbs and for these, due to the quantity you will use I would purchase these herbs from a Middle Eastern supermarket - ghormeh sabzi, sabzi polo, shivin (dried dill). You can buy them fresh and do all the chopping yourself or you can use a combination of both. Most commonly used are dill, coriander, fenugreek, parsley and leeks.

Oil and Salt - I generally use olive oil in all my cooking now, however coconut oil is a good alternative. I always use fine milled salt for Iranian cooking, and it is used extensively!

So that is it! Not as vast as you would imagine and with the addition of some pulses like kidney beans and broad beans and a protein source, you are ready to start your Persian cooking!

Nooshe jaan!

Advieh

I had a bit of a kitchen disaster a few weeks ago. I had completely run out of advieh! This is possibly the worst thing that I can imagine running out of at this time, not just because autumn has arrived, and all I want to do is eat huge bowls of khoresht whilst wearing PJs and slippers (the uniform of the working from home community!).

I only really discovered this spice blend around five years ago and now I cannot do without it. Without any exaggeration, I think that I use it in around seventy percent of my meals during any given week.

Advieh is akin to garam masala and ras el hanout in Persian cooking, in that it is a spice blend that differs by household and is used in a variety of dishes. I particularly love it with lamb, dry or in a khoresht. Either works well for me.

My last batch came as a present from my uncle, following his trip to Iran, and it is by far my favourite version. He said that there were literally hundreds of different blends of advieh and colour choices in the bazaars, which is amazing considering that every version that I have bought online or in a Middle Eastern food market and in the United Kingdom has just four ingredients, cinnamon, rose, cumin and cardamom.

The one that he gave me has twenty-four different spices in it but alas, it doesn't give me the exact quantities of each! I have scoured the internet and I found nothing that comes even fractionally close.

So, I decided to make my own and surprisingly I love the flavour of it and the depth and the variety of taste that comes through. It is relatively easy to make so, if you want to try it, please do, and let me know what you think!

Advieh

Ingredients:
½ teaspoon of ground saffron
1 teaspoon of ground chilli powder
½ teaspoon of black pepper
1 teaspoon of ground coriander
½ teaspoon of ground fenugreek
1 tablespoon of cinnamon
1 teaspoon of garlic powder
½ teaspoon of nutmeg
1 teaspoon of ground, dried rose petals
1 teaspoon of dried lemon
1 teaspoon of ground ginger
½ teaspoon of ground fennel
2 teaspoons of turmeric

Method:
Blitz all the ingredients together in a small grinder and store in an airtight container.

This should keep for three months.

Nooshe jaan!

Persian New Year – Nowruz

As the days are getting longer and warmer, spring is so close that I can almost taste it! Everyone is starting to dry their washing outside; children are playing in the gardens after school and everything just looks and feels a little bit better in general than the wet, drizzly, post-Christmas dark nights that January and February have to offer.

Another thing I love about this time of year is that one of my favourite Iranian festivals is just around the corner. Nowruz, or Norooz, is the Iranian New Year festival, that lasts for around two weeks. It literally means 'starting a new day' and is the celebration of the start of spring for all the reasons above!

Traditionally, us Iranians celebrate this festival with family and friends, and we spend the time celebrating the people we love, whilst talking about all our favourite moments from the year gone by and the things that we are looking forward to for the following year.

There are a few other traditions that come with Nowruz that I am rather partial to, one of which is a full spring clean (khāne-takānī). I have just this week started a new Jones family tradition. I started a little 'memory jar' for us all to put little notes inside about all the lovely things that we did throughout the year that we are thankful for, so that on New Year's Eve and at Nowruz we can read them out and celebrate all the best bits of the past year.

Finally, as with all Persian and Iranian gatherings, it would simply not be a celebration if it didn't involve food!

It is traditional to serve seven different dishes on the sofreh (a special cloth). The seven dishes are said to represent rebirth, health, prosperity, happiness, patience, joy and beauty. One of these is asheh reshteh which is a traditional noodle, bean, chickpea, mint and spinach soup. The noodles are meant to symbolise life's different and many paths.

My mum always used to make me an Iranian soup very similar to this whenever I was poorly and she used to add barley to it. I still to this day think that there was some kind of magic in it, as it always made me feel better!

I have my husband's family coming for the weekend to celebrate with us this year and I have decided to do a green herb menu to bring good luck for the coming year. I cannot wait to start preparing and cooking and to have the house full of lovely smells, colours and family.

Sabzi polo mahi - rice with fish and herbs to symbolise rebirth. I also ate mahi-mahi on my wedding day, so this will bring back some lovely memories. My husband had barracuda, but I doubt that I will be able to get hold of any of it this side of Shropshire!

Kuku sabzi - a green herb and egg tortilla (I used to hate this as a child as it is quite bitter, but I absolutely love it now).

Lavash - flatbreads.

Mast-o-khiar - a cold cucumber and mint soup.

Yakh dar behesht - an orchid ice cream or 'ice in Heaven', used for nourishment.

Baklava - to represent prosperity.

Sohan - a sweet saffron almond brittle to symbolise light and love for the coming year.

A Pinch of This and a Pinch of That

One of the things that I love about cooking and Persian food is that anyone can create something beautiful that will nourish you with as little as two ingredients. Is it a science? Some chefs say so.

Catering college trains chefs on the classics, where every single element is so precise that when finished it is utter perfection. But what about instinct? Does instinct have a place in modern-day cooking? I ask.

Okay, some of us have a natural ability and some of us need a lot of training, but is that not true of most skills, trades and vocations? I am not a chef. I am a wife, a mummy, a field marketer and I love food! I love eating it and I absolutely love cooking it!

The notion that 'real' cooking is a science seems alien to me and relatively frightening, as I'm pretty sure that I flunked science, or I may have scraped through with a 'C' in some kind of new mixed sciences.

I loathe following instructions generally and the thing that I mostly struggled with when starting my blog is that I want to share mine and my family's food with as many people as I can reach. However, I rarely weigh or measure anything, and my cooking is so far from being scientific that it's almost religious.

When baking, I decide what ingredients to use, based on how I want the cake to taste and what texture I am going for. If I am looking for a cake that is moist and rich, I will opt for oil instead of margarine, baking fat or butter. If I am looking for sticky and decadent, I will add sour cream or yoghurt, and the same goes for my cooking.

So many people have asked me how I cook my rice. It's hard to give a recipe that says something along the lines of 'add water up to your first knuckle on your index finger, add salt until it's salty enough, and oil to look about the size of the palm of your hand!'

Is anyone interested in that kind of recipe? It's how I learnt to cook. I used to watch the pressure cooker filling with ingredients without anything being measured, just instinct, practice and tasting at each stage.

When chatting to a friend about this and the fact that I am deconstructing every meal to weigh and measure things, she suggested that I write it down as I go.

So, as a bit of a test, I'm going to share one of my quick recipes in my own way and if anyone gives it a go, I would love to know how you get on!

Mast-o-khiar
(Persian cold cucumber soup)

The Iranian's absolutely love cucumbers and they will eat them like apples. My uncle and my dad used to have a bowl of mini cucumbers on the table and a little bowl of salt that they used to dip them in, which I am told is quite common in most Iranian households. My little sister now does the same.

There are so many different versions out there for this little dish, but this is the way that I have been making it for years and it is super simple.

Some people put raisins in it, some use a mixture of Greek yoghurt and natural yoghurt, and some use garlic. I tend to keep mine simple and I never use raisins as my husband dislikes any form of dried fruit.

Below is my recipe for mast-o-khiar which is delicious. It is like a minted cucumber yoghurt and it is really fresh, I make it to go alongside practically every rice dish.

Mast-o-khiar
(Persian cold cucumber soup)

Serves: 4
Preparation time: 10 minutes

Ingredients:
Low fat natural yoghurt
A small handful of finely
diced cucumber
A dash of dried mint
A few springs of freshly
chopped mint
A little chopped walnut
A few ice cubes and a
sprinkling of dried rose petals
and walnuts to decorate

Method:
Slice it all up and mix together.

Serve it with anything! (It's delicious.)

Nooshe jaan!

Starters

Starter

❦

Root Vegetable and Chickpea Falafel Recipe

Serves: 2
Cooking time: 25 minutes
Preparation time: 10 minutes

Ingredients:
2 cans of chickpeas in water drained and rinsed
1 red onion, finely chopped
2 garlic cloves, thinly sliced
1 teaspoon of cumin seeds, crushed
1 teaspoon of sumac
1 teaspoon of baking powder
2 raw beetroots (or equivalent amount of any other root vegetable), peeled and coarsely grated
A large pinch of salt
A large pinch of pepper
3 tablespoons of olive oil to brush
Shredded salad leaves, flatbread or pitta and mast-o-khiar to serve

Method:
Pre-heat the oven to 180°C fan, 190°C/375°F non-fan, gas mark 5.

Add all the ingredients, with the exception of the salad, pitta and mastokhiar, into a food processor and blitz to a coarse paste.

Tip into a bowl and season with salt and pepper and mix together.

Spoon the mixture into ten medium batches and squeeze them into egg shaped balls. (I think these look prettier than small round ones and it keeps the moistness locked in).

Brush a large roasting dish with olive oil and heat for a few minutes.

Add the falafel, drizzle with the remaining oil and roast for 20 to 25 minutes, turning once after 15 minutes. They are ready when they are golden brown, and the centre is warm.

Serve in a warm flatbread with salad and mast-o-khiar.

Nooshe jaan!

Root Vegetable and Chickpea Falafel

I only really discovered falafel when I started working in Watford. It has always been something that I have avoided, as it would have little or no flavour. Let me also just clarify that when I say falafel I don't mean the dried up little balls that you get in the supermarkets, that feel as if you are eating the Sahara when you bite into them. I mean real falafel, falafel that is moist and full of flavour and the ultimate guilt-free comfort food.

One of my colleagues always surprises me with falafel when I get into the office after a five-hour drive and, as I am totally enamoured by food, it instantly cheers me up, regardless of what joys the M6 had in store for me en-route.

Try this recipe and you'll be a falafel convert; I promise. Add some fresh lavash (flatbread) and mast-o-khiar (cucumber and mint yoghurt) and you will have a mezze for any surprise guests who arrive.

Kuku Sabzi Recipe -
My little Persian Green Omelette

I used to hate kuku when I was a child. It was way too bitter for me and I avoided eating it at all costs. Nowadays I love it! And it is made even better by the fact that it is healthy too! No carbs, no MSG, no naughties and so yummy!

Kuku is a type of omelette, similar to an Italian frittata, and it is filled with fresh chopped herbs. You can also make it with pre-chopped and dried herbs, but my preference is fresh.

Traditionally, this yummy green omelette is cooked over hot coals. Nowadays, however, an oven is just fine!

It is great served as a side dish or as a starter with salad, yoghurt and bread. Yep, yoghurt and an omelette!

I know that it sounds odd but trust me it works. Kuku is delicious hot or cold and it is great for picnics.

Traditionally kuku is eaten at Nowruz - Persian New Year and it is said to signify rebirth and fertility for the new year to come.

There are a thousand different variations of this recipe. I hope that you enjoy it as much as I do. Nowruz Mubarak to all of my wonderful readers.

Starter

❦

Kuku Sabzi Recipe
My little Green Persian Omelette

Serves: 6
Cooking time: 20 minutes
Preparation time: 15 minutes

Ingredients:
2 tablespoons of olive oil
1 large white onion peeled and sliced
6 free range eggs
1 teaspoon of baking powder
1 tablespoon of advieh
1 teaspoon of salt
1 teaspoon of black pepper
½ teaspoon of turmeric
2 cloves of garlic peeled and sliced
2 spring onions finely sliced
1 cup of fresh chopped parsley
1 cup of fresh chopped coriander
1 cup of finely sliced dill
1 tablespoon of plain flour

Method:
Add all of the olive oil to a heavy bottomed pan and place over a medium heat.

Add in the onions and sauté until clear and sweet. Remove from the pan and allow to cool.

Whisk the eggs with the dried spices and set aside.

Sauté off the chopped herbs until the bitter smell has gone.

Add the onions back into the pan with the herbs.

Turn the heat down to a low simmer. Pour in the egg mixture and cook with a lid on for about 15 minutes on the lowest level until set.

Place under a grill on a medium heat to brown the top.

Transfer into a serving dish and garnish with fried barberries and onions.

Serve with bread and mast-o-khiar.

Nooshe jaan!

Starter

Lovely Little Persian Lamb and Advieh Filo Straws

Makes 10 to 12 straws
Cooking time: 25 minutes
Preparation time: 5 minutes

Ingredients:
200 grams of left over leg of lamb or minced lamb (left over payeh bareh, chopped finely, works brilliantly)
1 finely diced onion
1 tablespoon of advieh
1 teaspoon of sumac
12 ready-made filo pastry sheets
1/3 cup of butter
3 tablespoons of olive oil

Method:
Pre-heat the oven to 180ºC fan, 190ºC/375ºF non-fan, gas mark 5

Slice the filo pastry into quarters and cover with a damp cloth until ready to use.

Add the olive oil to a pan and fry off the onions until clear.

Add the mince or the finely chopped lamb and fry off until brown (or hot to touch if using left-over meat).

Add the advieh and the sumac and fry for a further minute.

Take off the heat and leave to cool.

Melt a third of a cup of butter.

Slice the filo pastry into 4" squares.

Using a pastry brush, coat a sheet of filo pastry with a thin layer of butter and place a heaped teaspoon of the lamb mixture onto the middle.

Fold the filo over until it is all tucked in and looks like a straw.

Butter a further two sheets of filo, wrap the parcel twice more and place onto a greased baking sheet.

Repeat until all the pastry and the lamb mixture has been used.

Brush the pastry lightly with olive oil.

Bake in the pre-heated oven for 20 minutes, turning once halfway through cooking.

When the pastry is golden brown, remove and serve. These are delicious with mast-o-khiar or with natural yogurt, with some chutney stirred into it.

Nooshe jaan!

Lovely Little Persian Lamb
and Advieh Filo Straws

I went out for something to eat in Watford with some friends. We went to a lovely little Lebanese restaurant.

We had around ten different mezze plates and on one of these were some little lamb pasties.

They were so delightful that when I got home from my trip I decided to play around with some ingredients and some leftover leg of lamb, to make my own version for our weekend guest.

I decided on filo pastry instead of the shortcrust pastry that you would normally use for a little dish like this, because I love the crunch and the lightness that filo pastry gives you, and all the flavour is given to the filling, instead of the pastry being the main event.

Instead of opting for my usual fragrant spices, this time I went for depth and warmth; I used sumac and advieh. These two spices, when they are combined, are wondrous!

Needless to say, these little beauties didn't hang around long and even my guest who doesn't eat lamb ate two of them. So, I would say that they were a success and that they will make an appearance again soon!

These are so quick and easy to make, and they are definitely worth a try.

Salad Olivier

This lovely, essentially fancy potato salad originates in Russia and it is a party favourite of mine and of most Iranians! You will find it on the table at nearly every social gathering or party and it will nearly always be decorated with vegetables that have been made to look like flowers. My parents used to make roses out of tomatoes. To this day, although it's extremely kitsch, the thought of that still makes me smile.

Like most Persian dishes, there are many different variations of this. Even within my own family we all make it differently. This version is my favourite though. You can adapt it as you like by adding carrots, removing the Dijon mustard etc, to your own taste. There are no real rules to this other than that you must eat a lot of it and love it!

Iranians absolutely love to use oodles of mayonnaise in this dish; they take it even further with the mayonnaise love affair and they layer it on top, which can get a bit sickly.

So, I have adapted my own version to suit my taste buds and that of my mayo hating husband, who incidentally loves this dish as much as I do. From our table to yours. I hope that you enjoy this as much as we do!

Nooshe jaan.

Starter

Salad Olivier

Serves: 6
Cooking time: 20 minutes
Preparation time: 15 minutes

Ingredients:
4 medium sized white potatoes, peeled and chopped into 1cm cubes, boiled until cooked
2 medium sized hard-boiled eggs, chopped into small cubes
1 cup of garden peas, cooked
3 large gherkins, chopped into small cubes
3 spring onions sliced finely
1 cooked chicken breast, chopped into small cubes
½ cup of capers
½ cup of natural yoghurt
½ cup of mayonnaise
1 tablespoon of olive oil
1 large tablespoon of Dijon mustard
1 teaspoon of dried tarragon
Salt and pepper to taste

Method:
Mix all the ingredients together in a bowl and serve with warm flatbreads! Decorate with a tomato if you feel the urge!

Easy peasy and delicious!

This will keep in an airtight container in the fridge for around a week.

Nooshe jaan!

Starter

❦

Torshi

Serves around 20
Preparation time: 30 minutes.
Waiting time: 6 months to 15 years and beyond!

Ingredients:
1 Kilner jar
12 whole garlic bulbs
Two thirds of a cup of dried barberries
750ml of clear pickling vinegar

Method:
Sterilise your Kilner jar.

Peal the outer husks off the garlic but leave whole.

Clean the barberries.

Add all the garlic and the barberries to the jar, and pour over the vinegar.
Close the jar and leave it at the back of your cupboard or in a dark room for at least six months before using.

The longer the better. My uncle has one that is twenty years old and it's amazing! I love it with fresh lavash and kebab or côtelette.

Nooshe jaan!

Torshi

The Iranians enjoy pickled foods with most stews, rice dishes and kebab. You will find some wondrous and often unusual pickled foods in Iran, from garlic to walnuts and even fruits like melon. I have never tried pickled melon and I am not sure I want to, but I absolutely love pickled garlic. I love garlic in any form to be honest.

I had an interesting garlic ice cream once in Riga and I'm not entirely sure that I would eat that again, however I can highly recommend torshi!

The word torshi means 'pickle' and it comes from the Iranian word sour. Iranians are not huge fans of heat from spice, so their pickles are usually much milder than most Indian pickles and you will find that most are flavoured beautifully with seeds, berries and herbs. The key with any torshi is generally that, just like wine, the older the better. Some recipes will tell you to leave them for ten to fifteen years before eating, which takes some serious pickling commitment, I can tell you!

The recipe below is a simple but tasty garlic pickle, spiced with barberries, which are a sour Persian cherry like berry.

You can buy barberries from Amazon or from any Persian or Asian food market.

Sweet Potato Rösti with Poached Eggs

Sundays, in my humble opinion, should forever be a day of rest! I become very grumpy if I have to leave the house before midday on a Sunday or if I have to change out of my pyjamas pre ten a.m.! Thank goodness, the postman doesn't work on Sundays!

We live in a sleepy little North Shropshire town where most of the shops are closed on a Sunday, thus reinforcing my resistance to actually 'doing' anything other than playing with my four-year-old, eating brunch or cake and drinking coffee.

Today, I think that we are going to have brunch, a walk round the lake and spend the afternoon with friends and cake.

I haven't always had a predilection towards sleepy towns and quiet Sundays. Before meeting my husband, I lived in the middle of a beautiful city and my Sundays were mostly spent recovering from a Saturday night out or having brunch out in the city, amidst all the hustle and bustle of Norwich's lanes and streets, with my group of friends.

This tradition of wanting Sunday brunch hasn't changed despite me leaving the city and moving to a little 'backwater' town.

One of my favourite things to do on a Sunday still is to have Sunday brunch. Now though, instead of being in the middle of a city, it is spent having a lazy morning with my boys, in the comfort of our lovely home, listening to Madeleine Peyroux on the Sonos, drinking strong coffee (Nespresso Arpeggio is my choice of Java on a Sunday) and all of us in pyjamas!

Quite often, we have friends over for Sunday brunch and these little sweet potato röstis are a lovely twist on the traditional hash brown, making a great addition of flavour and spice to the norm.

I am partial to an element of spice with my breakfast and these have a perfect balance.

Starter

❦

Sweet Potato Rösti
with Poached Eggs

Serves: 2
Cooking time: 15 minutes
Preparation time: 10 minutes

Ingredients:
2 sweet potatoes – peeled and grated
1 white onion – peeled and grated
2 eggs
½ teaspoon of cumin seeds
½ teaspoon of advieh
Pinch of salt and black pepper
1 teaspoon of coconut oil

Method:
Pre-heat the oven to 180ºC fan, 190ºC/375ºF non-fan, gas mark 5.

Combine all the ingredients into a bowl (apart from 1 egg and the coconut oil) and mix together with your hands.

Heat a teaspoon of coconut oil (you can use 1 tablespoon of olive oil instead) in a heavy bottomed pan.

Shape the mixture into patties, flatten and fry off until golden before transferring to a preheated oven for 15 minutes.

Whilst the röstis are cooking, bring a pan of water to a boil and crack the remaining egg into it.

I do not add anything to the water when I make poached eggs and neither do I stir. I literally crack the eggs in and leave them bubbling away until the white is firm then remove with a slotted spoon.

Serve in a bowl with some rocket and a mug of strong coffee!

Nooshe jaan!

Starter

⚘

My Little Persian
Pistachio Pesto

Serves: 4
Cooking time: 15 minutes
Preparation time: 5 minutes

Ingredients:
50 grams of pistachios
1 small handful of fresh basil
leaves
3 garlic cloves
3 tablespoon of olive oil

Method:
Put all the ingredients into a blender and mix until it forms a paste.

Add to cooked pasta, fresh fish, salad or new potatoes and enjoy!

You can keep in a sterilised jar in the fridge for a week

Nooshe jaan!

My Little Persian Pistachio Pesto

A lesser known fact ... I am a cheese hater! So, ordinarily I avoid pesto unless it's homemade. This recipe is totally dairy free and so it's great for my vegan and dairy free friends, oh and not forgetting my fellow cheese haters! This recipe combines two of my all-time favourite cuisines, Italian and Persian. The sweet and the delicate flavours of pistachio nuts against the aromatic and intense flavour of fresh basil is a marriage made in heaven.

This yummy pesto is delicious on pasta, drizzled on fresh fish or salad or mixed into warm new potatoes. It's even great on flatbreads before you grill them, to pimp them up a bit! It honestly couldn't be easier, and I promise that once you make your own homemade pesto you will never buy shop bought pesto again.

Red Pepper Hummus

One of the first things that I gave my son to try when he was a baby after weaning was some homemade hummus with cucumber and he still loves it now. He gets it everywhere, but he loves it.

Not to brag, but my hummus is good. It has everything that you would expect from a good hummus.

It is garlicky, smoky, creamy and in no way at all dry, dense or sticky.

It is also super easy to make, and it keeps for at least a week in the fridge and it is cheaper than shop bought hummus.

So, a few tips when making your own hummus. Don't use dry chickpeas. I always use tinned chickpeas. They are pre-soaked, which saves a lot of time and they are by no means inferior. Use plump fresh lemons and roast the garlic or the peppers first.

Using raw garlic gives it a bit of a sharp taste and what you want from this lovely creamy dip is something warm that has a depth of flavour not a sharp one. Use the water that the chickpeas are in. I mean, aqua faba is used for meringues, naturally it will help give you a smooth, not grainy, hummus.

Starter

❦

My Little Persian Hummus

Serves: 2
Cooking time: 30 minutes
Preparation time: 10 minutes

Ingredients:
1 tin of chickpeas
3 cloves of roasted garlic
1 roasted red pepper with seeds and stalk removed
Juice of 1 lemon
2 tablespoon of olive oil
A bit of the water that the chickpeas are soaked in
Pine nuts and paprika to decorate

Method:
Put everything into a food processor and blitz until a smooth paste is formed.

Put into a bowl and sprinkle paprika and pine nuts over.

Get some warm bread and crudités and start dipping!

Nooshe jaan!

Starter

My Little Persian Potatoes

Serves: 4
Cooking time: 45 minutes
Preparation time: 10 minutes

Ingredients:
6 or 7 Maris piper potatoes - peeled and chopped into 1.5 inch chunks
1 teaspoon of salt
1 teaspoon of cumin seeds
1 garlic bulb – cloves with husks removed
1 teaspoon of smoked paprika
1 teaspoon of chipotle chilli flakes
1 tablespoon of plain flour
A good glug of olive oil

Method:
Pre-heat the oven to 200ºC fan, 240ºC/475ºF non-fan, gas mark 9.

Blanch the potatoes for 5 minutes in boiling water with the salt.

Add the olive oil to a roasting pan and put in the pre-heated oven for 5 minutes.

Drain and shake the potatoes in the pan with the lid on until they all look a tiny bit dishevelled.

Add the remaining ingredients to the pan and shake again until coated.

Pour into a roasting dish, be careful as the oil will be hot and may spit at this point.

Cook for 35 to 45 minutes shaking a few times in between.

Nooshe jaan!

Garlic and Egg Soup

Nestled on a mountain roadside on the C77 in Valenciana en route to Guadalest (which can only be described as a bare-knuckle car drive if you have a nervous disposition like me) is this hidden gem of a restaurant, El Riu Guadalest.

We have visited this eatery several times before and its charm never fails to amaze us. Greeted with warmth and a smile, we are quickly shown to our table overlooking the valleys of the dramatic mountain range that we drove through.

We opted for the daily special for just €14 and we eagerly awaited our feast! What a feast! What we thought would be a light lunch turned out to be a four-course meal with wine!

The hostess bought baskets of bread, aioli, potatoes and a tomato, aubergine and bacalao dip so tasty that it was gone in seconds!

Next, and the star of the show for me, was this understated, rustic garlic soup!

Oh, my word! It had bits of garlic skin floating around in it, a few poached eggs, some crispy croutons and a clear consommé broth that was packed with oodles of flavour! It was amazing! So much so that I immediately asked for the recipe.

This was then followed by garlic chicken, which had basically every part of the chicken in a bowl. I was already full by this point, but as usual the glutton in me took over and I finished it all.

It was 30ºC outside and I was both fit to bursting and a bit tipsy because of the huge carafe of wine that the lovely lady gave us, so I opted for an ice cream dessert instead of one of the amazing array of Catalan desserts on offer, all included in the price!

Our little boy had mountain sausages and potatoes and he eagerly devoured every morsel!

We came to pay the bill and it was less than €33 for all of us!

That amazing feast was mind-blowingly good value, but best of all was the flavour of the food and the warm service that we received, in the most beautiful setting, far away from the ordinary tourist spots.

It was just perfect. We will be back again! Well done El Riu Guadalest, what a gem you are! So, as this soup was amongst one of the top twenty things, that I have eaten in my life I felt the need to share the recipe with all my readers!

I hope that you enjoy it as much as I did!

Starter

❦

Garlic and Egg
Soup Recipe

Serves: 2
Cooking time: 180 minutes
Preparation time: 5 minutes

Ingredients:
4 whole garlic bulbs
Around 2 litres of water
1 tablespoon of salt (add
more if required)
Sourdough bread, cubed,
fried in 4 tablespoons of olive
oil and then baked until hard
Free range eggs, poached
2 tablespoon of olive oil

Method:
Get a big cooking pot. One that you would normally make a casserole in.

Add the olive oil to the pot.

Fry the garlic, skin on, until golden brown and just soft.

Add the water and salt and boil away until the broth turns brown but stays clear (this part can take around three hours).

Taste. If it tastes garlicky and salty it's ready.

Add freshly cooked poached eggs and sour dough croutons and enjoy!

Nooshe jaan!

Starter

❦

My Little Persian Indulgence – Baghali Ghatogh

Serves: 1
Cooking time: 10 minutes
Preparation time: 5 minutes

Ingredients:
2 cloves of garlic
1 cup of shelled broad beans
1 teaspoon of turmeric
¼ teaspoon of ground
cardamom
2 tablespoons of dried dill
2 organic eggs
1 tablespoon of olive oil

Method:
Add the olive oil to a heavy bottomed sauté pan and set to a medium heat.

Add the garlic to the pan.
Sauté the garlic gently until softened.

Add the shelled broad beans. Fry for 2 mins.

Add the turmeric and fry off until it no longer smells bitter.

Add the ground cardamom.

Add the dried dill and fry for 1 minute, then add the egg on top. The heat of the beans will cook the egg through.

Enjoy with white rice or chunky bread.

Nooshe jaan!

My Little Persian Indulgence – Baghali Ghatogh

After nearly falling into the canal on my run and straining my calf muscle, I needed some quick and yummy comfort food ... enter baghali ghatogh!

This five-minute simple dish reminds me of when I was a small child. It's so intensely garlicky and creamy and when served with some white Basmati rice and tahdig that makes it my all-time favourite indulgence for a super quick fix!

Salad Shirazi

I love telling stories. This is something that you may have guessed if you follow my blog.

However, when I find something funny, it is a well-known fact that I have an inability to tell a story without laughing hysterically, thus rendering me completely unable to complete my story telling.

Since I was nine years old my sister, my brother and I used to spend Christmas Eve at my dad's place.

We always had a big meal, consisting of ghormeh sabzi, lubia polo, salad olivier and salad shirazi, amongst a few other yummy things.

My dad would spend two days cooking for us ahead of this and the house would be full of noise and food all day. It was lovely.

The first Christmas that my husband and I shared I decided to take him to my dad's. We were all sitting round the table and as usual we were all swapping dishes and passing them around.

My sister passed my husband a dish and he turned to me and he whispered, 'What is this?'

So that you are aware, I am now laughing as I type, as the dish that he was asking about was a bowl of my dad's salad.

Yes salad!

I wondered if I had miss heard but nope, he asked me again and I ever so politely replied, 'Salad!'

I then turned to my dad in hysterics telling him that my new and lovely Welsh boyfriend (at the time) didn't know what salad was.

Every time I tell that story now my husband gets all defensive and he tells me that he was asking if it had a special name. Well he was kind of right, it does in fact have a name other than plain old salad.

It is salad shirazi and the recipe follows.

Starter

Salad
Shirazi

Serves: 4
Preparation time: 10 minutes

Ingredients:
1 Whole Iceberg lettuce
(optional)
4 Salad tomatoes
1 Cucumber
2 Red apples
1 White onion
2 tablespoon of Lemon juice
1 teaspoon of Dried mint
1 teaspoon of Sumac
1 tablespoon of Olive oil
Salt and pepper to taste

Method:
Chop, mix, drizzle, eat!

Nooshe jaan!

Starter

❦

My Little Persian Flatbreads

Makes around 4 flatbreads
Cooking time: 1 minute on each side
Preparation time: 10 minutes

Ingredients:
250 grams of self-raising flour
250 grams of natural yoghurt
½ teaspoon of baking powder
1 teaspoon of nigella seeds
1 tablespoon of garlic olive oil (you can also use plain olive oil)
1 lime

Method:
Mix all the ingredients together and knead into a ball on a floured surface. Divide into 4 balls.

Place back into the bowl and cover with cling film for 15 minutes.

Lightly cover a griddle with the garlic olive oil.

Roll out each ball separately until around ½ centimetre thick.

Cook for around two to three minutes. Turn once until golden on both sides.

Drizzle with lime or a garlic and herb olive oil and serve with khoresh.

Nooshe jaan!

My Little Persian Flatbreads

I love summer. I love all our seasons and how different they all are. I am however one hundred percent more suited to autumn than to summer for several reasons:

1. I do not cope well in the heat! I overheat constantly and I spend a good few months with a very shiny face!

2. I really love food - in case you hadn't guessed – which means that my waistline ninety-nine percent of the time is non-existent, which is difficult in the summer, with all the summery dresses and the sheer tops. I am much more suited to big baggy jumpers and jeans that keep everything where it should be!

3. I love spice! And huge big bowls of comfort food that make you 'ooh' and 'ahh' as soon as you smell them cooking! Yet another argument in the 'yayyy' box for jumpers!

4. I turn into a sloth when the clock ticks past seven p.m. at night! So, in summer when everyone is still out and about 'enjoying' the lighter nights, I secretly want to be snuggled up by a big roaring fire in my PJs with a huge bear like blanket over me, eating something.

So, as this week has slowly become more autumnal as every day passed, I am dusting off my tagine pot and I am getting my bread making hands ready. I am a bread fiend!

I love anything bready. Flatbreads, bread rolls, barm bread, sourdough, rye bread, cobs, champagne pave, thick chunky white sliced bread. Any form of bread that can be dipped into something yummy!

These little Persian flatbreads, although not exactly traditional, (but then I don't own a brick oven) are so ridiculously easy to make and they are delicious dipped into a tagine or a Khoresht or soup.

There is nothing tricky about them. A relatively common recipe with some minor alterations. They take under thirty minutes to make from scratch and they require very little kneading.

Give them a go. You can add any seeds or ingredients that you want to them. They work well with nigella seeds and roasted garlic pressed into them also!

Meat

Meat

❦

Payeh Bareh
(Persian Leg of Lamb)

Serves: 4
Cooking time: 5 hours
Preparation time: 30 minutes

Ingredients:
For Dusting:
1 teaspoon of turmeric
1 tablespoon of plain flour
A pinch of salt and pepper

Marinade:
1 sliced white onion
3 garlic cloves sliced
1 teaspoon of advieh
1 cup of water
1 tablespoon of runny honey
Juice of 1 orange and the grated rind
½ teaspoon of saffron (ground with a teaspoon of sugar and dissolved in 1 tablespoon rosewater)
1 tablespoon of coconut oil
The all-important leg of lamb! You can use the shoulder also; however, for this dish I prefer the leg.

Method:
Melt a tablespoon of coconut oil into a heavy bottomed pan or Dutch oven.

Pre-heat the oven to 150°C fan, 165°C/320°F non-fan, gas mark 3.

Rub the dusting into the lamb and fry off. When golden, remove from the pan (this should take around five minutes max).

Place the lamb into a deep roasting dish. To the frying pan add the rest of the ingredients and bring to a gentle boil. When boiling pour over the lamb and cover with foil.

Cook for around 5 hours basting every hour until the last hour then baste every 15 minutes.

Garnish with sliced pistachios and pomegranate.

I love this best served whole, on a table, for everyone to pull a piece off (it falls apart so there is no need to slice anything) with a big plate of baghali polo (broad bean and dill rice).

Nooshe jaan!

Payeh Bareh (Persian Leg of Lamb)

I work in Central London mostly. As I walk down Carnaby Street, I am always quickly surrounded by the general hustle and bustle of the city. I notice all the eateries around me, something that I have grown to take for granted and that I expect as one of the pleasures of everyday life now.

One of the things that I love about working in the city when I get chance to get down there, (I say down as I live on the North Wales and the North Shropshire border) is the absolute abundance of choice that this city offers for something to eat!

From mini pancakes with Nutella on the corner of Hanover Street, to a shop front in Camden that sells great beer and a lobster in a bucket with a basket of fries, to a stunning restaurant in the clouds serving delicious sushi, Kobe beef and even more delicious cocktails!

But ... this hasn't always been the case. If I go back a few years ... (and I wish that it was only a few) to conversations in the school playground around what we all ate for dinner the previous evening, I always felt like the odd one out.

My parents cooked amazing Persian food and I grew up eating things that most of the children who I went to school with had never heard of. My friends used to come around for dinner and they would be amazed at what they called 'shiny rice', which my sons both now call 'scratchy rice'!

I'm ashamed to admit that until my early adult years I took this for granted and I never really understood what a beautiful gift this was.

And then things changed. Cultural food diversity happened, and more and more choice became available. Today, we are lucky enough to live in a society where you can sample tastes and sounds from different cultures just by crossing the road.

A country's food has often so much to do with the heart of that culture and the nation and no more so than Persian food.

Love and care is the echo in every Persian dish, from methodically washing the rice until the water runs crystal clear to spending days cooking a feast for your family, because to really taste the flavours you need to give the delicate ingredients time to develop.

They say that the best Persian food you will eat is in a Persian's home. I don't know who 'they' are but they are certainly correct! This is true for all the reasons above. The time it takes, the love that goes into it and each individual take on every dish. If you have yet to try any 'real' Persian food, I cannot urge you enough to give it a go. You won't be disappointed.

Meat

Persian Milk
Chicken

Serves: 4.
Cooking time: 3 hours
Preparation time: Overnight

Ingredients:
1 whole large free-range chicken
1 teaspoon of turmeric
1 pomegranate - de-seeded
1 white onion peeled and sliced
3 garlic cloves peeled and sliced
2 preserved lemons
1 pint of whole milk
Salt and pepper to taste
1 teaspoon of cumin seeds
Pistachio slivers to decorate

Method:
Cover the chicken in the dry spices and place it in the fridge overnight or for a few hours prior to cooking.

Crack the back of the chicken and place in a tagine clay pot.

Pour the milk over the chicken and add the garlic, lemons and onions and cook on 150ºC fan, 165ºF/320ºF non-fan, gas mark 3 for 3 hours, basting every hour.

Make sure that when you take off the tagine lid to close your eyes and take a deep breath and imagine yourself sitting in a Persian bazaar surrounded by beautiful colours, smells and noise.

Drizzle the juices over the chicken before serving.

Decorate with pistachio slivers and pomegranate seeds.

Serve with rice and salad or chunks of fresh bread.

Nooshe jaan!

Persian Milk Chicken

This Persian Milk Chicken is delightful and so easy to make during the week when you are busy, or like this evening, when it's been a busy week and you just want something yummy but low maintenance! It goes perfectly with a huge salad and some chunky bread or a big bowl of rice and tahdig! This chicken has a delicate citrus tang to it which is complemented by the warmth of the turmeric and the background heat of the cumin. Scrumptious!

Happy Chinese New Year!

Chinese and Persian New Year have some similarities. Both are celebrated on a different day each year. Chinese New Year follows the lunar calendar and the Persian New Year marks the coming of Spring.

Both are very familial occasions, and both use food to symbolise luck, family, wealth and health.

Ordinarily I cook a Chinese feast to mark the occasion and to teach our little boy about other cultures and the world around him. Although he learns a lot from me and my family being Persian and my husband being Welsh, we live in a small town in North Shropshire and so it is important to us that he understands cultural diversity in all its glory.

This year, however, instead of doing the normal noodles and dumplings, I am playing with the similarities between the festivals and I am relating it to the food that I am going to cook. I am taking some yummy Chinese meals and I am fusing them with my Persian roots, one of which is my little Persian shredded lamb pancakes (see the recipe below).

Happy Chinese New Year! I hope that it brings all my readers health, happiness, prosperity and peace.

Meat

❦

My Little Persian
Shredded Lamb Pancakes

Serves: 4
Cooking time: 5 hours
Preparation time: 15 minutes

Ingredients:
1 shoulder of lamb
1 red chilli sliced and de-
seeded
4 cloves of garlic
A good glug of olive oil
(around 4 tablespoon)
½ sliced cucumber
Seed of 1 pomegranate
4 spring onions
20 Chinese pancakes
½ pot of natural yoghurt
2 teaspoons of dried mint
Pomegranate molasses
Flatbreads or pancakes

Method:
Pre-heat the oven to 220°C fan,
240°C/475°F non-fan, gas mark 9.

Cover the lamb in olive oil, rock salt,
chilli and garlic and cover in tin foil.

Cook for 30 minutes.

Remove and baste and reduce the heat
to 150° fan, 165°/320°F non-fan, gas
mark 3 and cook for 5 hours, basting
every hour.

While the lamb is cooking slice the
cucumber, the spring onions, the
deseeded chilli, and the pomegranate
and place into small dishes in the fridge
for serving.

Mix the mint and the yoghurt together
and place it in the fridge until ready to
serve.

When the lamb is cooked, remove and
shred. Make sure that you shred all the
rendered fat also as this adds to the
flavour.

Place in a serving dish in the middle of the table with the flatbreads, molasses, the yogurt, cucumber, pomegranate and spring onions and let everyone dig in and build their own pancakes!

Nooshe jaan!

Meat

Cotelettes

Serves 4:
Cooking time: 30 minutes
Preparation time: 15 minutes

Ingredients:
1½ waxy peeled and cooked
potatoes - mashed
500 grams of minced beef
1 medium white onion peeled
and grated
1 teaspoon of turmeric
2 teaspoons of salt
Pepper to taste
½ teaspoon of ground saffron
½ teaspoon of cinnamon
1 teaspoon of garlic granules
2 small eggs beaten
150 grams of breadcrumbs
Salad, mast-o-khiar and
lavash to serve
2 tablespoon of olive oil for
frying

Method:
Mix all the ingredients together, except for the breadcrumbs, in a big bowl for around five minutes.

Place the breadcrumbs onto a spare plate.

Spoon a ball of the meat mixture into your hands and roll into a log shape.

Add the olive oil to a frying pan set over a medium heat.

Flatten into an oval, cover in breadcrumbs and place in the hot frying pan.

Cook for 2-3 minutes on each side.
Place in the oven at 150°C fan 300°F/ gas mark 2 to keep warm while you cook the rest.

Don't overcrowd the pan or touch them too much until they are fully cooked on each side.

Place on a paper towel to drain and serve.

Nooshe jaan!

Cotelettes

Although the name suggests 'lamb cutlets' these couldn't be further from them. They are little potato and saffron meat patties that look like little hamburgers but taste like Kebab.

They can be served with rice and salad or with hot fresh lavash. I enjoy them both ways and I can eat them by the dozen!

My most nostalgic memory of these delicious little beauties is eating them hot straight out of the pan in my dad's kitchen! He still makes the best ones I have ever had but mine come a close second.

One of our dear friends ate so many at one of our dinner parties (despite my husband warning him that we had three more courses to get through, one of which was basically a kilo of rice each) that he had to do diaphragm stretches in between courses whilst walking around the garden!

He also really struggled with their name and although I cannot write down what he called them; trust me it was an amusing afternoon dinner party!

For all of these reasons, these little patties will always be a firm favourite of mine and they will always make me smile.

Sumac and Garlic Meygu

I was a fussy eater growing up. I would refuse to eat meat and I made my dad pick out all the bits of meat from any khoresht that I was having. I wouldn't go near fish and I hated all manner of dairy.

I wish sometimes, that I was a fussy eater now!

The truth is that except for butter, salmon and cheese I eat everything! And generally, a lot of everything, which does nothing for my waistline! But here is the thing, I love food! Shellfish is a favourite, of mine especially langoustine or Giant Atlantic King Prawns!

I do not remember when I first started eating shellfish or why. Neither my parents nor my siblings eat shellfish so I can only assume that I developed the taste for it as an adult.

Whatever it was, I love it! There is not much, in my opinion, that beats a plateful of grilled giant Atlantic king prawns that have been marinated in garlic, lemon, chilli and sumac, served with chunks of crispy white bread and a garlic yoghurt dip!

I am getting hungry typing and my mouth is starting to water!

These little gifts from the sea could not be easier or more delicious! Try them and let me know what you think.

Meat

Sumac and Garlic
Meygu

Serves: 4
Cooking time: 3 minutes
Preparation time: 10 minutes, marinate overnight

Ingredients:
1 kilogramme of Giant Atlantic Prawns
2 teaspoons of sumac
5 garlic cloves
1 lemon
½ red chilli - deseeded and sliced

Method:
Marinate overnight with all the ingredients.

Get the gas barbecue nice and hot! Cook them for around 3 minutes.

Serve with chunks of French bread and aioli!

Nooshe jaan!

Meat

⚘

Persian Lamb and Advieh Flatbread

Serves: 4
Cooking time: 15 minutes
Preparation time: 15 minutes

Ingredients:
For the Base:
75 grams of Greek yoghurt
350 grams of plain flour
150ml of warm water
2 tablespoon of olive oil

For the Topping:
500 grams of minced lamb
2 finely sliced garlic cloves
1 teaspoon of turmeric
2 teaspoons of red advieh
1 finely sliced white onion
1 tablespoon of Pine nuts
150gm of Greek yoghurt
2 teaspoon of dried mint
1 small bunch of fresh sprigs
of mint and coriander
1 tablespoon of Pomegranate
seeds
2 tablespoon of olive oil

Method:
Make the base by combining the ingredients and knead until you have a round ball of dough.

Leave to settle in a clean bowl covered in cling film, while you cook the topping.

Add the oil to a good sized frying pan and set over a medium heat.

Fry off the onions and garlic until clear.

Add the lamb, remove from the heat and put to one side.

Now portion off the dough into four balls and roll out into four flat pizza bases.

Add plain flour to the work surface and use a rolling pin to stop it from sticking.

Add a bit of olive oil to a heavy bottomed pan and fry off for about 30 seconds on each side.

Next, add your lamb mix to the base.

Drizzle with olive oil and place in the oven for 10 minutes until the crust starts to bubble and brown.

Whilst this is cooking, mix the dried mint with the remaining Greek yoghurt and set aside.

Remove from the oven and dollop with Greek yoghurt, sprinkle with pomegranates, pine nuts and the fresh herbs, slice and serve!

Nooshe jaan!

Persian Lamb and Advieh Flatbread

Have you ever noticed how a plane goes quiet when you are about to take off? I recently travelled to Rome for work and as I wasn't wrestling with my little boy to keep him in his seat or plying him with raisins and stories, I had the chance to take in my surroundings. It was very quiet.

I absolutely adore Rome. It is arguably in my top five cities to visit for so many reasons, one of which is the food. Not the only reason. Just one of them.

Italian food has so many similarities to Persian food in the way that it is prepared and enjoyed. Both with passion and conversation!

The Italians love to serve huge bowls of amazing tasting food to enjoy with nice wine and great company. Both of which no meal should ever be without!

I always say that Persian food is best eaten with large groups of people. Every mealtime is a social event. My husband and I often just put a pot on the table and share whatever I have made with a fork and a glass of wine each. We did exactly that tonight as I wrote this page!

As with most of my favourite meals, my favourite Italian meal comes with a story. Mostly, the food that I love is not just about the flavour. Obviously, the flavour is paramount, as is the enjoyment of a lovely view, great ambience and conversation. If, however, the food is rubbish, then it won't be high up on my list of inspirations or a meal to recreate.

However, the ones that stand out most, do so because all the elements of a great meal have come together and etched it in my memory.

My first experience of Rome was when my husband took me away on my thirtieth birthday for a week. I loved every second of this beautiful city! We took in all the sights; Did all the touristy and non-touristy things and then we ate.

We shared a Diavola pizza and a carafe of red wine at the base of the Colosseum. It was the most perfect meal. Simple, delicious and I remember smiling a lot!

On my most recent trip, (and having seen all the sites before) with only an hour of spare time, I simply sat and refreshed my memory whilst enjoying my pizza and watched the old city in full flow. It was utter bliss for that stolen slice of time.

So, in tribute to my travels of late, I have been inspired to create a Persian/Middle Eastern pizza/flatbread. I hope that you enjoy it as much as we did.

From my table to yours!

Meat

❖

Joojeh Kebab

Serves: 6.
Cooking time: 30 minutes
Preparation time 10 minutes, marinate for up to 3 days in advance of cooking

Ingredients:
1 kilogramme of skinless, boneless, chicken thighs
2 limes
2 white onions
1 teaspoons of ground saffron
2 cloves of garlic
1 teaspoon of rosewater
1 cup of natural yoghurt
½ cup of olive oil
1 teaspoon of sea salt
½ teaspoon of pepper

Method:
Place the chicken thighs into a bowl or a plastic container that has a lid.

Slice the onions and garlic and add to the bowl.

Juice both limes and add along with the ground saffron, rosewater, yoghurt, olive oil and salt and pepper.

Get your hands dirty and mix it all in. Cover and refrigerate for at least 24 hours. I like to marinate mine for at least 48 hours before cooking to let the flavours really permeate the meat.

You can either skewer them or add them flat to the grill. I prefer mine on a flat skewer that you can slice off at the table. It's a real crowd pleaser. I use the dark meat for this, as it is moist and delicious.

Cook for around five to seven minutes turning continuously to ensure that they are cooked through and serve with fresh lavash and salad.

Nooshe jaan!

Joojeh Kebab

The arrival of this lovely weather that we have been having lately has encouraged my husband to give his barbecue a bit of TLC. This outdoor grill has had lots of attention.

They have spent hours together in the garage, catching up about how much they have missed each other, how cold it has been, and how cooking indoors just isn't the same as the lovely smokiness that you get from an outdoor grill.

He has given it a complete overhaul in the last few weeks, from newly painted woodwork to new burners and lava rocks and, as such, it has repaid us by cooking to perfection some lovely meals.

I love barbecue season and I will happily eat outdoors every single night of the week in the summer months; something which does tend to happen from May through to September in our household!

Thankfully I have a husband who shares my passion for anything grilled and he will gladly don his barbecue apron and tools and set about cooking whatever I have marinated for us.

I have such lovely memories of barbecues at my aunt and uncle's in Suffolk when I was a small girl. We used to get in the car at the crack of dawn, it always felt like such an adventure travelling for what was only two hours, but it felt like a whole day back then.

The planning that used to go into a trip was incredible, considering that nowadays I regularly drive a seven to eight hour round trip to work if I am needed in the office for a day, without thinking anything of it.

I always used to love my uncle's Saffron Chicken and my dad always used to say how much he enjoyed it and that it was worth the drive just for that!

On this occasion, the whole family went. My cousins and I spent a good deal of the day just playing in the garden, watching the grownups chat, cook and laugh.

I will never forget this occasion because it was the time when one of my cousins bit into one of those delicious chicken drumsticks and then realised that the chicken was still raw!

I just remember lots of movement and the slightly undercooked chicken being swiped out of his hand straight away and him looking a tad confused. It was hilarious! I still laugh about it now when I make these and that was a good twenty-nine years ago (at least)!

Needless to say, he didn't get salmonella or anything of the kind and my dad to this day always pre-cooks chicken in the oven before sticking it on the barbecue!

If, like me, you love grilled chicken and saffron, I urge you to try these. This is simply the best way to cook and to enjoy chicken flat wings or thighs!

Meat

Persian Lamb
Kebabs

Serves: 4
Cooking time: 15 minutes
Preparation time: 20 minutes

Ingredients:
500 grams of minced lamb
20% fat
1 onion grated
1 egg beaten
Flour added to aid binding
and stickiness
Salt and pepper to taste

Method:
Mix everything together in a large bowl for ten to fifteen minutes until sticky.

Take a sausage size amount and place it around the skewer until it covers it. Pinch the ends onto the skewer.

Dip your hands in a bowl of water between each kebab. Repeat until you have used all the mixture.

Place on a rack on the barbecue for five minutes turning and basting every 30 seconds.

Serve with hot fresh lavash or basmati rice and sumac with a barbecued tomato on the side. Either way works perfectly!

Nooshe jaan!

Persian Lamb Kebab

Am I the only one that thinks that we seem to be a society that loves the next big thing?

The plant-based, fifteen-minute, fitness conscious, clean eating trends seem to be the thing now.

It seems that everywhere I look people are dieting, cutting back and going raw this, steamed that, with some chia seeds thrown in for good measure.

I often sit and wonder where these things start and what is it that makes everyone start spreading avocado on toast. I liked that trend and I still do it with a splash of lime and some fresh chillies.

One-minute people are juicing up shots of wheatgrass (hated that trend) and the next they are flossing quinoa out of their teeth.

I remember when it was all about goji berries! I have never been one for following trends. Not food or fashion really. I am all for balance, everything in proportion and eating a well-rounded diet and not overindulging every day.

Equally though, I love real food; food that makes you go 'mmm' when you take that first bite and when you realise that you are going to enjoy every mouthful of what is on your plate. Isn't that what food is all about? Surely it isn't just fuel? It should be enjoyed, savoured, appreciated and remembered!

Well this recipe is one of those 'mmm' moments. When you taste it, it makes you smile from the inside out.

If you ask most Persians what their favourite food is, I can bet most will say either chelo kebab or ghormeh sabzi!' Persian kebab are worlds away from the awful dry things that you can (but don't, hopefully) buy on sticks at the supermarket.

They are juicy, melt in your mouth and delicious. The key is not in the ingredients, but in what you do with the ingredients to get them to hold the shape and to retain the moisture the way that these do.

Some tips before you try ...

Use wide flat skewers as the meat holds better on them. I got mine from Amazon.

Don't put them directly onto the barbecue grate as they will stick and then you will have to scrape them off, which ruins them entirely! Melt butter in a pan beforehand and brush it on to the kebabs as they are cooking. Turn regularly (every thirty seconds or so).

When mixing the lamb mixture, mix for ages until it gets really sticky. This breaks the fibres of the lamb down, but it also aids them sticking onto the skewers properly. I have been let down so many times because I haven't mixed it long enough, or I haven't got them sticky enough and they just fall apart.

If you have a barbecue coming up be sure to do the above and your guests will keep coming back for more!

Meat

ᛦ

Chicken and Olive Tagine

Serves: 3
Cooking time: 2 - 3 hours
Preparation time: 15 minutes

Ingredients:
Olive oil
2 large onions
4 large garlic cloves
1 teaspoon of ground coriander or coriander seeds
1 teaspoon of ground ginger
1 teaspoon of cumin seeds, toasted first
A handful of pancetta cubes
150 grams of olives
100 grams of capers
5 preserved lemons or 2 fresh lemons
1 heaped teaspoon of caster sugar to sweeten
2 tablespoon of olive oil
A pinch of saffron threads pounded with a teaspoon of sugar dissolved in ½ cup of hot water
6 to 8 large boned skinless chicken thighs. You can use breast, but I prefer the dark meat in this dish

Method:
Pre-heat the oven to 140ºC fan, 150ºC/300ºF non-fan, gas mark 2.

Make the dry rub by mixing all the dry ingredients together in a bowl and coat the chicken thighs with it.

Heat the oil in a heavy bottomed pan, fry off the pancetta cubes and add the marinated chicken.

Cook until the chicken has turned golden.

Add sliced onions and garlic and fry for three minutes.

Next add the preserved lemons and a cup and a half of water.

Add the olives, the sugar, the saffron fluid and the capers and transfer to a tagine/clay pot.

Add the lid and cook for around two hours.

When ready, remove from the oven place straight on the table and serve with polo ba tahdig, lavash (bread) or a lovely green salad.

Garnish with pomegranate and pistachio slivers or sliced candied lemons.

Enjoy the aroma when you remove the lid for the first time.

Nooshe jaan!

Khoresht

I was with a friend this week. We were discussing our impending birthdays and it made me think about my own, and the lovely tradition that my husband started years ago. This tradition involves a lazy weekend and a tagine; both of my favourites! I used to wonder what all the fuss was about concerning a tagine. It always takes hours and is it worth it?

The simple answer is yes! Not only are they beautiful to look at, but the minute you open a tagine, your senses are delighted with so many different aromas and colours. If you close your eyes and breathe in, you can almost imagine yourself sitting in a bazaar on a cushion surrounded by noise, colour and delicious fragrance and flavour.

The clay tagine (lid) is magical in how it works. You simply fill it with water and allow the clay to absorb the water for ten to twenty minutes before cooking. It then slowly steams away whilst absorbing the aromas and the flavour.

Each time you cook with it you will taste something different. It is without a doubt one of my kitchen aids that I could not do without.

The first time I tried this dish was on my birthday, six or seven years ago when my lovely husband spent a day cooking for me. It is always such a treat to be cooked for, especially by him, as he completely understands the love and the care that I put into every meal I cook, and he does so equally when preparing this for me.

He still cooks this every year for me on my birthday (apart from my thirtieth when he took me to Rome where we ate pizza and drank carafes of red wine) and it has become a lovely tradition, one that I so look forward to. It is also one of the most delightful ways to eat chicken that I have ever tried.

From our table to yours, I hope that you enjoy it!

Meat

My Daddy's
Ghormeh Sabzi

Serves: 6
Cooking time: 4 hours
Preparation time: 30 minutes

Ingredients:
6kg of lamb shanks or 3kg of diced lamb. I use shanks and slice the meat after, leaving the bones in for flavour. (My dad and my uncle eat the marrow out of the bones which still to this day makes me feel queasy).
3 medium white onions diced
3 dried Omani limes pierced
3 big handfuls of chopped or dry sabzi (parsley, leek, coriander and fenugreek)
1 bag of washed fresh spinach finely sliced
1 garlic clove
1 glug of olive oil
1 tablespoon of turmeric
A generous pinch of salt and pepper
2 tins kidney beans
3 tablespoon of olive oil

Method:
Add the olive oil to a big stewing pot over a medium heat or a pressure cooker.

Fry the onions and garlic until clear.
Add the turmeric and fry off for a few minutes, stirring continuously to get rid of the bitterness before adding the meat.

Add the meat and fry gently until browned, then add the chopped fresh spinach and fry off for five minutes, stirring the whole time.

Add the sabzi and the lime and continue to stir.

When it is all fried and you can start to smell the herbs cooking, add the water up to a third of the pan.

If using a pressure cooker, cook on full until the pressure hits and it starts to hiss, then on low for thirty minutes. If using a pan, cook slowly for two hours, then add the kidney beans.

Leave overnight and reheat the following day if possible.

Serve with polo ba tahdig and salad shirazi.

Nooshe jaan!

My Daddy's Ghormeh Sabzi

I remember the first time when I made this, I had just moved into my own house. My dad had given me a pressure cooker for my birthday and I decided to try to make ghormeh sabzi.

Well! I had no idea how to use a pressure cooker and I managed to take the lid off before the pressure had been released.

Big mistake! It exploded! Literally hit the ceiling, removing the vile artex, and showering the entire kitchen, my dog Phoebe and me with a bright green sauce! It looked like Popeye had been through the kitchen in a tornado of spinach!

Thankfully, over the years, I have worked out how to use one and it hasn't happened since. There are literally hundreds of different versions of this out there, however my dad's version is still my favourite. I have adapted his recipe a tad. I hope that he will approve!

So, what is ghormeh sabzi? If you ask any Persian, they will tell you that ghormeh sabzi is the most iconic of herb stews and it is akin to an English roast dinner in its significance. It is full of fresh herbs and it can be made with either lamb or chicken. It is unlike any other dish, stew or tagine that I have ever tasted. It is fresh, with sharpness and warmth at the same time.

In my version, instead of using lamb chunks I prefer to use whole lamb shanks, as the bones add to the flavour of the whole dish. I always cook this at least twenty-four hours ahead of eating and if possible forty-eight hours as it tastes so much better when the flavours have had the chance to mature. If you have never tried it, have a go at making it. It really is worth the effort and with all the spinach in, it is great for you too!

Khoresht Ghameh

Omani limes are like Marmite. You either love them or hate them. I happen to love them, however, I ordinarily, believe it or not, have more of a savoury tooth than sweet and normally I lean towards a bitter and sharp flavour preference.

Omani limes originated in the Persian Gulf and they are completely dried out and have lost all their water content. You can use them whole, sliced or ground. I always use mine whole and pierce them. They are delicious in khoreshts and tagines (stews).

In Persian cooking, these limes are used to add a sour flavour to a dish such as a soup or a stew. You can buy them from most good Asian food markets, and I have also managed to buy some online.

Sadly, I have yet to see any in the UK supermarkets though. However, that may just be down to the area that I live in. They have an intense sour and smoky flavour. My favourite dish to cook them in is a Persian stew with potato chips and beef - khoresht ghameh.

Khoresht ghameh, as all Iranians will testify, is a completely indulgent stew with chips and served with rice! so, carb dodgers be warned! It is worth having an extra-long run for though, just to indulge in this.

When we have Persian dinner parties, my carb loving husband always asks me, 'Can you make the one with chips?'

Meat

Khoresht Ghameh
(The One with the Chips)

Serves: 4
Cooking time: 3 hours
Preparation time: 30 minutes

Ingredients:
2 cups of Olive oil
2 onions sliced
500 grams of stewing beef
Juice of 1 lemon
1 whole lemon sliced in half
2 garlic cloves
1 whole garlic, skin on and
top sliced off
1 teaspoon of turmeric
150 grams of yellow split
peas
2 cups of water
4 Omani limes pierced
½ teaspoon of cinnamon
400 grams of tomato passata
1 tablespoon of tomato puree
½ teaspoon of saffron
threads ground with a
teaspoon of sugar and
dissolved in a tablespoon of
hot water
2 waxy potatoes peeled and
chopped into chips

Method:
In a heavy bottomed pan, fry off the onions in the oil until clear.

Add the turmeric and fry off until the bitter smell goes.

Add in the meat and cook until browned. Next add lemon juice and let it sizzle before adding the garlic.

Add in the whole lemon and whole garlic When fried off add in the tomato puree and fry off for 30 seconds.

Add the passata and hot water, the pierced Omani lime and the cinnamon.

Add in the split peas and cook on a low heat for around 3 hours or transfer to a slow cooker and cook on low for 6 hours.

Meanwhile peel and fry chips until crispy.

When the stew is cooked, remove from the heat and stir in the saffron liquid.

Transfer to a bowl and place a stack of the chipped potatoes on top and serve with tadig and rice.

Nooshe jaan!

Meat

⚘

My Little Persian Aubergine Stew - Khoresht Bademjune

Serves: 4
Cooking time: 3 hours
Preparation time: 20 minutes

Ingredients:
2 large aubergines
2 lamb shanks or 500 grams of stewing lamb
2 large white onions sliced
juice of 1 lemon
4 garlic cloves - sliced
2 heaped teaspoons of turmeric
1 teaspoon of ground cinnamon
1 teaspoon of salt
Pepper to taste
400 grams of tomato passata
½ tube of tomato puree
2 cups of hot water
1 cup of sour grapes, sliced in half
½ teaspoon of saffron threads pounded with a teaspoon of sugar and dissolved in 1 tablespoon of rosewater
1 cup of olive oil

Method:
Add ⅓ cup of olive oil to a frying pan.

Peel and slice the aubergines and add to the pan.

Fry them off until cooked through. Place to one side.

In a heavy bottomed pan add a good glug of olive oil and fry off the onions, until clear and softened.
Add the meat and brown off.

Add the garlic and cook for 3 minutes.

Add the lemon juice and let it sizzle before adding the turmeric, tomato puree, salt and pepper. Fry off until the bitter smell disappears.

Add the passata and water and stir.
Lastly add the cinnamon and place a lid on the pan and cook for around 3 hours on a low heat.

15 minutes before serving add the aubergines and the saffron liquid and decorate with sliced grapes.

Serve with polo ba tahdig and fresh lavash!

Nooshe jaan!

My Little Persian Aubergine Stew - Khoresht Bademjune

I do love escaping every now and again and switching off entirely, but I also love coming home, especially to lovely autumnal weather. It makes me crave massive bowls of comfort food, packed with oodles of flavour!

We holidayed in Barbados and while we were away, we ate out in lots of different restaurants. We ate some amazing fresh fish and a variety of really colourful food. One thing that we noticed was that the island's signature dishes were offered in most of the eateries that we visited.

Each one of them offered a slight variation in the ingredients, in the way it was prepared and then presented. It got me thinking about regional food in general. There must be thousands of different versions of how to make a chicken korma, fish and chips, pad Thai, jambalaya, and the list goes on.

The same is true of Persian food. Within my own immediate family, we all make ghormeh sabzi, salad olivier and sholerzard differently. They all are identifiable as the actual dish with the core ingredients being similar; however, we all have different palates, and we have adapted to our own tastes over the years and, of course, we all think that our own version is the best! Mine is actually the best, for any of my family who are reading this.

This is true for most Persian dishes, from cakes to stews and the way that we cook rice. There is one common element to every dish across every Persian households, though. We love the food and the process of cooking it for our friends and our family.

Here is my own version of khoresht bademjune. This was my ultimate favourite as a child and it always felt like such a treat. It is still a firm favourite in my own family now and I hope that it remains that way for generations to come.

From my table to yours.

Meat

Khoresht Kadu
My Little Pumpkin Stew

Serves: 4
Cooking time: 3 hours
Preparation time: 30 minutes

Ingredients:
2 tablespoons of coconut oil melted
2 large onions diced
750 grams of chicken thighs on the bone
1 teaspoon of turmeric
1 teaspoon of ground cinnamon
1 tablespoon of plain flour
750 grams of diced pumpkin flesh - fried off until browned
2 tablespoons of soft brown sugar
Juice of 2 limes
½ teaspoon of ground saffron with a pinch of sugar and dissolved in warm water
½ cup of pomegranate seeds

Method:
Fry off the onions in the coconut oil until soft. Set aside.

Coat the chicken thighs in the flour and dried spices.

Add to the onions and fry off for 1 minute.

Pour in ½ a cup of water and simmer for around 45 minutes.

Add in the sugar, lime, saffron and pumpkin and cover and simmer for another 45 minutes until the pumpkin is soft.

Season to taste with salt and pepper and serve with tahdig and rice.

Decorate with pomegranate seeds and coriander.

Nooshe jaan!

My Little Pumpkin Stew

I love the crisp clear mornings and the chilly nights that arrive with Halloween. We have always celebrated Halloween. Even as a small child my mum used to throw the best Halloween parties.

One year, I think I was around seven years old, she threw a party for us and all my school friends came. The food that she made was so scary that none of the children would eat anything!

The standard of costume back in the eighties, for us at least, was a binbag over our clothes and our faces painted green.

Nowadays, it is very different! Some of the social media posts that I've seen of friends celebrating this year looked amazing and a far cry from the old binbag witch that I used to go as!

In Iran today, many of the younger generation, under thirty-five, who make up seventy-five percent of the population, do indeed celebrate Halloween, despite the clear risks.

They do so away from the watchful eye of the police, and they demonstrate their knowledge of Western culture and traditions.

At the request of our little boy, we always decorate our house with cobwebs and make Halloween snacks and he loves all of the theatre surrounding it.

My husband, not so much! However, we do have a tradition that we have had since we met and that is picking our pumpkins and then carving them in competition with each other!

I am pretty sure that I have won more times than

I've lost, but who's counting? I love this tradition. It is something that we now do with our little ones.

My mum used to use the pumpkin flesh to make khoresht kadu and my dad would sit and pick all the seeds out, dry them, methodically cover them in salt and bake them.

I haven't thought about that in years, neither have I done it myself! They are lovely, yummy and crunchy and a nice alternative snack for this time of the year.

Khoresht kadu, the way I make it, is sweet and sticky and I find that it works better with the dark chicken meat rather than any other meat.

However, you can also use beef or lamb. If you are vegetarian you can replace the meat with potato, chickpeas and broad beans, which also works well.

It's warming and perfect after a cold autumn day. So, if you are struggling to think of ways to use all that leftover pumpkin without making a pumpkin pie or a soup, try this! You won't be sorry that you did.

Rice

Y

My Little Lamb and
Apple Khoresht

Serves: 4
Cooking time: 180 minutes
Preparation time: 20 minutes

Ingredients:
1 tablespoon of olive oil
2 large white sliced onions
500 grams of diced leg of lamb
2 cloves of garlic, peeled and sliced
400 grams of tomato passata
1 teaspoon of ground saffron, with a pinch of sugar dissolved in 1 tablespoon hot water
1 tablespoon of pomegranate molasses
3 Omani limes, pierced
1 apple, cored and sliced
1 white potato, peeled and sliced into rounds
2 carrots, peeled and sliced
½ butternut squash, peeled sliced and fried off
1 cup of dried apricots
2 heaped teaspoons of advieh
1 teaspoon of turmeric
2 teaspoons of salt
1 teaspoon of ground black pepper

Method:
Preheat the oven to 160ºC fan, 175ºC/340ºFF non-fan, gas mark 4.

Add the oil to a heavy bottomed pan and set over a medium heat.

Add the onions and fry until clear.

Add the spices to the pan and fry off for one minute.

Add the lamb chunks and brown off.

At this stage add everything to a tagine pot along with the vegetables.

Pour the passata, molasses and the half cup of water into the pan with the spices and heat until it comes to the boil.

Pour the sauce over the meat and vegetables.

Add the saffron liquid and place the tagine lid on top.

Cook for three hours.

Serve in the middle of the table with forks, chunks of bread and good company!

Nooooooshe jaan!

My Little Lamb and Apple Khoresht

The genius of Persian cooking is that it is instinctive. Most of our recipes can be taken with the proverbial pinch of salt, due to differing subtleties and flavours of spices and seasoning. Everything is done to taste, and it takes practice and instinct to get it just right.

The beauty of this dish specifically is that it is so versatile. For my vegetarian and vegan friends and readers, you can omit the meat and switch the vegetables around to your liking. Just keep the core spicing and water content the same and you can't go far wrong. We Persian's call a stew a khoresht, although a khoresht for me is so much more than a bowl full of stew. It is a fusion of sweet and salty.

It has the ability, when you lift off the lid for the first time, to transport you to a souk or to a bazaar in the Middle East.

The smell of all the roasted spices, the beautiful colours and the wonderful delicate flavours of a Persian khoresht really reflect the country itself and make these pots of heaven some of my favourite comfort foods.

The garnishing and the decoration are equally as important as the core dish. The pistachios and the pomegranate jewels used to garnish most dishes, not only add beauty but also texture, and contribute to the sweet and bitter contrasts that are renowned in Persian food. It's a marriage of opposites that when bought together creates something quite magical.

Are they a quick fix? No. Certainly not. The secret ingredient to good Persian food is time and lots of it! It takes a lot of time and preparation but the result is always worth it. They make you feel warm and cosy when eating them!

And with all this chilly weather, we all need a little bowl of pick me up don't we?

Rice

Rice

Polo Ba
Tahdig

Serves: 4
Cooking time: 60-75 minutes
depending on colour of tadig
required
Preparation time: 10 minutes

Ingredients:

1 cup of good quality Basmati
rice per person plus an
additional cup for the pan.
For this recipe, I will use 4
cups.
Salt to taste
2 tablespoons of olive oil
Pistachio/sliced almonds and
rose petals to garnish

Method:
Use a good non-stick pan or an Iranian
rice cooker. A Western rice cooker will
not do for the tahdig (the crusty bit) as
they turn off at a certain temperature
and just continue to steam the rice.

Wash the rice until the water runs clear.
This removes the excess starch and any
impurities.

Once it's all clear empty the water.

Add a cup of water per cup of rice and an
additional cup of water for the pan. The
water should come up to approximately
an inch above the rice.

Add the salt to taste. This is quite a salty
rice traditionally. I usually use around ½
tablespoon of salt but I taste the water
and I add more if needed.

Add 2 tablespoons of olive oil.

If cooking in a pan, add to a hob on a
medium heat for around 30 minutes.
Once the rice starts to boil turn down to
a simmer for another 20 minutes or so.
You will know when the rice is done, as
it starts to smell like popcorn.

To turn the rice out of the pan, put the lid on and run the bottom under a cold tap then turn upside down onto a plate. If using a rice cooker, it is very easy. Just turn it on to your desired colour and when the light goes out it is done!

Decorate as you wish.

Nooshe jaan!

Polo Ba Tahdig

I read a post a while back on the BBC entitled Should I worry about arsenic in my rice?' It was an informative look by Dr Michael Mosley at the reasons why rice 'may' contain levels of arsenic.

He explained that, due to the way that rice is grown (flooded conditions), the arsenic that is locked into soil can be more easily absorbed into rice. He went on to explain that there are ways that we can reduce this risk and one is the way that we soak rice or cook it.

It got me thinking about the way that Persian rice is cooked and why our rice is so different. Apart from the obvious look and flavour differences of our rice, one of the main things that separates Persian rice from the rest is the way that we handle it before we get to the cooking and the eating stage.

When I was taught to cook rice, I was taught to wash it clean: to make sure that the water runs crystal clear in the bowl of rice before you add any seasoning to it or start cooking it, as this process washes away the impurities and makes sure that when it is cooked it remains as separate grains rather than a sticky sloppy mess. What I understand as an adult when I cook it, is that through this little bit of extra love and attention to cooking rice, it is a far safer way to cook it and it limits any dangerous bacteria and levels of the aforementioned arsenic by as much as eighty percent! A very good reason to wash your rice first!

Everyone who knows me knows that I am a self-confessed rice snob. One of the things that I really dislike is badly cooked rice; and rice with no flavour.

The absolute travesty of these is American long grain and those awful pre-cooked packet rice, which I am glad to say I do not possess and will never allow to darken my doorstep, let alone my plate!

These are the reasons why so many people misunderstand rice and see it as just a filler, the side or the support act.

Well, rice deserves more respect than that. Firstly, its story and legacy is one of utmost importance and it does not deserve to be just the bland accompaniment to your main dish.

Rice has provided food and homes for people for millions of years. Whole economies rely on its very existence. And secondly, cooked correctly it is delicious! Full of flavour and without a doubt the crowd pleaser of the meal!

Having said all that, I thought that I should add a little recipe for traditional white Persian rice. Better known as polo ba tahdig. Enjoy! Befarmaid.

Rice

Baghali Polo

Serves: 4
Cooking time: 60 minutes
Preparation time: 30 minutes

Ingredients:
4 cups of basmati rice
Salt to taste
1 cup of dried dill
1 cup of chopped fresh chives
3 cloves of finely sliced fresh garlic
2 cups of fresh shelled broad beans - I always use frozen and I defrost them before shelling, as they taste fresher and the colour is a much deeper green.
3 tablespoon of olive oil

Method:
Wash the rice until the water runs clear.

Add the herbs, garlic, salt and beans to the pan along with 1.5 cups of water to every cup of rice.

Add the olive oil and stir.

Stir and cook for 45 minutes until a tahdig forms.

Stir after 15 minutes to ensure that the herbs are mixed in with the rice.

Turn out and simply enjoy with a runny egg!

Nooshe jaan!

Baghali Polo

It was a Saturday afternoon and I had been feeling poorly. It must have been 1990 (I remember, as this was when Stars in their Eyes first appeared on our TV screens). My dad and I were sitting on our blue velour sofa (well he was, and I was sitting on his lap), in the front room of our flint house, watching Stars in their Eyes and shelling broad beans to make baghali polo. I loved doing this little task with him, especially as he used to let me eat the beans that I managed not to crush! It is surprising the damage that tiny hands can do to the beans when attempting to get them out of their shells!

Rice is the main staple in Persian cooking and baghali polo is a popular and a widely eaten variation. My version uses dried shivin (dill) alongside finely sliced fresh garlic and chives. The addition of the dried dill really seasons and deepens the flavour of the fresh herbs and adds a freshness to it that is great served with fresh fish or a rich khoresht.

As a child, this wasn't my favourite rice to eat as it can be quite bitter. However, as an adult I absolutely adore it. The shelling of the broad beans is therapeutic and a great fun way of getting my little boy to help cook. He loves it when they pop right out of the shell and go flying out of his hands, or equally when he manages to squish one or twenty! You can serve this with my payeh bareh (Persian leg of lamb) or simply with a crispy fried runny egg. There is no greater comfort food than that! The egg yolk acts as a rich, salty sauce to the rice and the flavours work perfectly. Simple and delicious.

Albaloo Polo -
Rice with Sour Cherries and Meatballs

This dish is utterly divine. It is indulgent and sociable, subtle in deliciousness due to the delicate spices used, none so overpowering that it prevents you from tasting each spice individually.

The rice becomes patchily stained by the juice of the sour cherries and the tahdig (crust at the bottom of the pot) is fragrant, with a syrupy sweetness about it from the saffron and the yoghurt. My husband tells me he can't get enough of this meal and that the meatballs, delicately flavoured with turmeric, are like sweets!

I haven't made this dish for years, as traditionally it should be made when the first sour cherries are ready for picking in Iran. However, I was chatting to my dad and he casually dropped into the conversation that he had made albaloo polo for my stepmother and it made my mouth water, so I set about looking for some sour cherries to make this!

The problem is, and it's not really a problem, with albaloo polo, is that I get red stained fingers from preparing the cherries and a tummy ache from overeating!

Once I taste the first mouthful of this meal something happens and the glutton inside of me takes over and before you know it, I am lying on the floor, groaning and begging for mint tea! - so worth it though!

Rice

Albaloo Polo
Rice with Sour Cherries and Meatballs

Serves: 4
Cooking time: 60 minutes
Preparation time: 25-30 minutes

Ingredients:
500 grams of fresh sour cherries - pitted and washed (I use Morello or sometimes I replace the cherries with barberries)
100 grams of sugar
4 cups of strong Basmati rice - washed until the water runs clear
1 tablespoon of cinnamon
500 grams of minced beef
2 teaspoons of turmeric
1 teaspoon of salt
2 garlic cloves
1 small red onion
2 tablespoons of natural yoghurt
½ teaspoon of saffron ground with sugar
1/3 cup of olive oil

Method:
Wash the rice until the water runs clear.

Add water until the rice is covered by around half an inch of water on top.

Add salt and two tablespoons of olive oil and cook with the lid on until all the water is absorbed.

Remove from the pan and set aside.
Add the cherries to a bowl and cover with the sugar.

Mix the saffron with the yoghurt and pour it into the bottom of the rice pan.

Start layering the rice on top, one layer of rice then one layer of cherries, then repeat.

After each layer of cherries add a sprinkling of cinnamon.
Repeat this step until all the rice and cherries have been used.

Place the lid back on the pot and cook for 40 minutes.

While the rice is cooking, make the meatballs.

Place the meat, garlic, onion, turmeric, salt and pepper into a food processor and blitz until smooth.

Bring a heavy bottomed pan on to the heat.

Add the rest of the olive oil and start rolling the meatballs into 1 penny sized balls.

Place in the pan and fry off until browned. Place in a heated oven around 180ºC fan, 190ºC/375ºF non-fan, gas mark 5 whilst you brown off all the meatballs.

When the rice is cooked, transfer it to a plate and decorate with the meatballs and the pistachio slivers.

I eat this with some fresh salad and mast-o-khiar!

Nooshe jaan!

Rice

Lubia Polo
Rice with Green Beans and Tomato

Serves:4
Cooking time: 120 minutes
Preparation time: 10 minutes

Ingredients:
2 medium white onions sliced
500 grams of minced steak
or diced lamb or beef
1 heaped teaspoon of
turmeric
2 garlic cloves finely chopped
2 tablespoons of tomato
puree
1 carton of tomato passata
2 cups of green beans - fried

½ teaspoon of saffron ground
with 1 teaspoon sugar and
dissolved in 2 tablespoons
water
½ teaspoon of cinnamon
Salt and pepper to taste
4 cups of basmati rice
5 tablespoons vegetable oil
or olive oil
1 cup of water

Method:
Add 2 tablespoon of oil to a pan and
add the sliced onions and fry off for five
minutes.

Add the turmeric and the garlic and fry
off for a few minutes.

Add the meat and cook until browned.

Add in the tomato puree and stir for a
few seconds before adding passata and
1 cup of water.

Season well with salt and pepper and
simmer for forty minutes.

Whilst that is simmering, slice the green
beans into one inch pieces and fry off in
a saute pan with 2 tablespoon of olive oil
until cooked through.

Add these to the simmering pan and
leave to cook for 60 minutes.

Add the cinnamon and the saffron liquid.

When this is cooked through, leave to
one side.

Wash the rice until the water runs clear

and add to a rice cooker.
Add water up to one cm above the rice, add the rest of the oil and season well with salt.

When the rice is starting to cook and the water has all been absorbed, remove it from the pan and rewash it. This stage is important as it will keep the rice separate and not stodgy and sticky.

Slice some potatoes and place them in the bottom of the pan with a drizzle of olive oil.
Meanwhile, mix the rice with the sauce that you made earlier and carefully scoop it all back into the pan.

Put the lid back on and cook for around 60 minutes, depending on how dark you like your tahdig (crispy rice at the bottom).

The tahdig should look a dark brown to black, due to the sauce in the rice, so don't be alarmed when you turn it out. It isn't burnt! This is exactly how it should look, and the darker it is the better it tastes, as anyone who has had it will tell you.

Turn out and serve with mast-o-khiar and salad!

Nooshe jaan!

Lubia Polo
Rice with Green Beans and Tomato

Lubia polo is my best friend's favourite Iranian dish and I always cook it for her when she comes to stay with us, as a treat. Her birthday is on the second of January and she always gets a bit moody (more than normal) at this time of the year. I think it's down to the fact that no one has any money after Christmas, and everyone is partied out, thus a birthday is a bit inconvenient.

A few years ago, her partner tried to surprise her with a trip to Chester Zoo and the surprise was that we would meet her there. Well, he made a terrible mistake bringing me in on the plan, as I got way too over excited by it all and nearly let the cat out of the proverbial bag! My hubby and I prepared a picnic. We got party hats, I made some chocolate cupcakes and some lubia polo to take along for her. We set it all up in the jaguar picnic hut and we had a lovely little party there.

Lubia polo is the perfect one pot meal for a family feast or for dinner parties. Its appearance is very dramatic with its dark tahdig, and it's great because you can make it ahead of time and then just throw it all in a rice cooker on the day and cook it, which means more time entertaining! And not forgetting the most important thing, it tastes amazing!

You can make lubia polo with diced meat or minced. I prefer minced with mine. You can add potatoes to the tahdig or do without and you can add some heat with a bit of cayenne pepper. It is also lovely as a vegetarian dish. Just omit the meat and add finely cubed aubergines for texture.

Desserts

Desserts

My Little Persian Pancakes

Serves: 4
Cooking time: 5 minutes
Preparation time: 5 minutes

Ingredients:
2 cups of plain flour
1 teaspoon of baking powder
1 free range egg
1 ¾ cups of whole milk
½ teaspoon of ground cardamom
1 tablespoon of vegetable oil for frying

Method:
Place all of the ingredients in one bowl and mix with a whisk for a few minutes until there are no lumps in the batter.

Heat a heavy bottomed skillet pan with a tiny bit of butter or oil.

When the pan is nice and hot, pour in spoonfuls of the mixture until the size of pancake desired is formed.

Heat until little air bubbles form.

Flip over to the other side and cook for around 1 minute or until golden.

Eat hot with a good douse of maple syrup!

Nooshe jaan!

My Little Persian Pancakes

We love pancakes here at My Little Persian Kitchen! But who doesn't? They are such a nostalgic treat and so versatile too. Sweet or savoury, scotch, crepes or buttermilk, I like them all. Every year as a child we would have pancakes for dinner on pancake day without fail. They would be plain with lemon juice and sugar, some with sultana's in, and some without.

Always hot and straight out of the pan, they always felt like such a treat. I mean, when else in the year can you legitimately eat cake for dinner? This variation is one of my favourites. They are super quick, crisp on the outside and fluffy in the middle, and perfect with a good drizzle of maple syrup or a glug of honey.

Yum! Happy flipping!

Desserts
❧

My Little Persian Granola Bar Recipe

Makes around 20 bars
Preparation time: 5 minutes

Ingredients:
1 cup of rolled oats
1 cup of rice crispies
½ cup of smooth peanut butter
½ cup of organic honey
¼ cup of cocoa
¼ cup of pistachios sliced
200 grams of dark chocolate

Method:
Melt the peanut butter and the honey together in a glass bowl and microwave for 45 seconds until smooth.

Add all the other ingredients, apart from the dark chocolate, into the bowl and mix until combined.

Spoon into a baking paper lined square cake tin.

Next, melt the dark chocolate in the microwave until runny. This normally takes 45 seconds and I stir halfway through, to avoid burning.

When completely melted, pour the chocolate on top of the granola and decorate with slices of pistachios.
Cover with cling film and put in the fridge to set.

When set, remove and slice.

Store in an air-tight container in the fridge for around 2 weeks.

Nooshe jaan!

My Little Persian Granola Bars

Spring is desperately trying to bloom here in North Shropshire. We occasionally have days that are full of promise of better weather to come and then it's quickly scuppered by a downpour!

Despite the weather, I am in full Nowruz preparation. We have our lentils soaking ready for the sabzeh to grow for Haft Seen.

We are planning our various menus for when we have friends over, and we have started making sweets! I love this time of year!

With Nowruz being so closely followed by Easter, I wanted to make some sweet snacks that weren't laden with refined sugar like most of the ones I make.

These little six ingredient granola bars are super easy to make, and they taste as if they should be bad for you.

However, they have no nasties and they are perfect for that mid-day indulgence.

If you try them out, please let me know what you think.

My Little Persian Cardamom Shortbread

I learned to make shortbread at Brownies. I must have been around eight years old and the first time that I made them I was proud as punch - not too dissimilar from now really!

I made lavender ones a few years ago and my lovely uncle said that they tasted like soap! Not quite as successful that time around. These are much nicer, I promise. They resemble noon nokhodchi in flavour, which is one of my favourite Persian sweets. However, these are a lot easier to make.

If, like me, you are a fan of cardamom, give this cardamom shortbread recipe a go. They are yummy, and they will last you a week if stored in an airtight container.

Desserts

❧

My Little Persian
Cardamom Shortbread Recipe

Makes around 8 – 12 biscuits
Cooking time: 20 minutes
Preparation time: 10 minutes

Ingredients:
250 grams of butter
110 grams of caster sugar
360 grams of plain flour
2 teaspoons of ground
cardamom

Method:
Heat the oven to 175ºC (fan assisted) 345ºF / gas mark 3

Line a loose bottomed tray with baking paper.

Beat the butter and the sugar together until smooth.

Stir in the flour and the cardamom with your fingers until a crumby consistency is formed.

Press into a shallow loose bottomed dish or baking tray.

Score into the shapes you want and press little holes into the dough with a fork and scatter caster sugar lightly on top.

Bake in the oven for 15 to 20 minutes, or until pale golden-brown.

Leave to cool and store in an airtight container.

Nooshe jaan!

My Little Summery
Persian Loaf Cake

Well, our hazy summer days have definitely come to an end and it has been anything but summery up here in North Shropshire for the last few weeks!

It seems that Shropshire has received the memo about autumn arriving.

I do love the lighter nights, the warmth of summer, and all the extra time that you have in any given day, but my favourite season is here now and I can't feel sorry about it, not even one little bit!

I am not quite ready yet to put aside my proverbial flip-flops just yet.

However instead, I've been playing around with some ingredients to make a cake that, I feel, tastes just like summer should, in order to say goodbye to the season that we have just closed off.

The best thing about it, apart from how it tastes, is the fact that it is pretty much one bowl, one spatula and it takes thirty minutes to make! No fuss at all!

It has everything that you would expect from a summer cake. It is bright with sunshiny colours, fruity, floral, fresh flavours, light and sweet; but I would say that, wouldn't I?

The ingredients that I have used are the ingredients that evoke memories of summer holidays with my husband.

Coconut - reminds me of the smell of suntan lotion and warm sand.

Oranges - countless glasses of juice with breakfast, with the sea in clear view.

Honey - the sticky sweet cakes and sweets that you often get in hotels.

And orange blossom because, well, it wouldn't be a cake of mine without some form of floral note added for good measure.

If you have friends over or you just feel like a little lift, please give my summer Persian loaf cake a try and let me know how you get on.

You won't be sorry that you did.

So, goodbye flip flops and salad and hellooooo, jumpers, wellies and big hearty tagines!

Desserts

My Little Summery Persian Loaf Cake

Serves: 6 – 8
Cooking time: 30 minutes
Preparation time: 10 minutes

Ingredients:
225 grams of self-raising flour
50 grams of desiccated coconut
100 grams of caster sugar
2 medium eggs
250ml of natural yoghurt
150ml of olive oil
Zest of 1 orange
1 teaspoon of ground cardamom
1 teaspoon of baking powder

For the Syrup:
100ml of water
100 grams of caster sugar or ½ cup of honey
Juice of 1 orange
2 teaspoons of good quality orange blossom syrup

For the Drizzle:
2 tablespoons of icing sugar
2 teaspoons of water

Method:
Pre-heat the oven to 140°C fan, 150°C/300°F non-fan, gas mark 2 and line the baking tin with parchment paper.

Combine the dry ingredients into a mixing bowl and stir.

Mix the eggs, yoghurt, oil, and zest together and then add to the dry ingredients.

Mix well until combined and place in the baking tin. Bake for around 25/30 minutes until golden brown and a skewer inserted comes out clean. Leave to cool in the tin for 15 minutes.

While the cake is cooling, poke tiny holes all over the top and make the syrup. Add all the ingredients to a pan and bring to a boil then reduce the heat until the mixture has thickened and reduced. This takes about 10 minutes.

When the syrup is ready, use a spoon and pour over the cake. Leave to settle for a few hours.

To make the drizzle, add the icing sugar and a few drops of water to a bowl and whisk with a fork until smooth and thick.

To Decorate:
Chopped pistachios
½ cup of icing sugar
Drop of water

Dollop the drizzle on the cake, spread it over the surface and decorate with sliced pistachios.

This is lovely on its own with a coffee or a cup of strong Persian Chai.

Nooshe jaan!

Desserts

Honey and Orange
Blossom Syrup Recipe

Serves: 4
Cooking time: 15 minutes
Preparation time: 2 minutes

Ingredients:
½ cup of sugar
100ml of water
1 tablespoon of organic
locally sourced honey
2 teaspoons of orange
blossom water

Method:
Add all the ingredients to a pan and simmer for around 15 minutes until reduced and thickened and sticky.

Great on pancakes, ice cream, over fruit or natural yoghurt or on waffles!

Nooshe jaan!

Honey and Orange Blossom Syrup

I watched a documentary on the honey trade the other evening. I am normally quite thick skinned, what a bizarre saying that is, I mean I'm sure that we all have the same thickness of skin and even if some of it were thicker than others why would it stop you from getting upset?

I wonder where that saying came from? One to Google later!

Anyway, I digress, where was I? Oh yes, honey!

So, I watched this programme and it was about the honey trade and basically what it amounted to was that a vast proportion of what we buy in the supermarkets, believing it to be honey, is mixed with some form of syrup.

Some rice, some corn and, worst of all, are the ones with hormones that are given to bees, which are dangerous for humans to consume; and don't even get me started on the criminal activities surrounding honey!

Full colonies of bees are being stolen and being left to die in America and all for what, an extra few pounds? It makes me feel incredibly sad when I watch programmes like this.

Such programmes as this unfortunately showcase some of the poorer behaviours that we as human beings undertake, and all in the pursuit of the shiny penny. Unwitting consumers then buy a product that isn't what they believe it to be.

I love honey. Yes, I do use the word love an awful lot when it comes to food; however, it is true. Honey has woven its way through my memories.

Some of my first memories were of tasting honey on

156

toast. When I had a cough as a little girl, my dad would make me hot chocolate with a tablespoon of honey in it and he would tell me that's what his mum, my mamanie, made him; although I am sure that he tried to convince me that she also used to crack an egg in his! The honeyed hot chocolate always got rid of my cough and my sore throat and it still does to this day.

I love desserts as sweet as you can handle, all doused in a honeyed syrup and then, as I grew into adulthood, honey in my tea and mixed into natural yoghurt or straight from the honeycomb with a thick cream and fresh hot lavash for breakfast, for no other reason than I love the flavour.

Now, as a mummy myself to a gorgeous cheeky little boy, I use honey when he is poorly, in smoothies, on a teaspoon as 'sweetie medicine' and, if he has a sore throat, on cuts and scrapes or as a treat with yoghurt.

The thought of it not being real honey and being a syrup of some kind or a product of some despicable criminal activity is sad.

I was blissfully unaware of the things that this programme highlighted. One of the many reasons that I actively avoid television is because it never fails to disappoint me, and it makes me question why we do the things that we do. Maybe I am oversensitive, or maybe naïve.

I know that the honey crisis is just one of another million other things that as human beings we must add to our 'things to concern ourselves with' list, but, as of now, before I ever buy honey again, I am making sure that it is local honey, not blended and one hundred percent pure!

So, as an ode to my honey rant above, I have made this gorgeous honey and orange blossom syrup to douse my breakfast pancakes in. You're welcome!

Desserts

❦

My Little Persian
Spiced Chocolate Cake

Makes around 12 slices
Cooking time: 25 - 30 minutes
Preparation time: 5 minutes

Ingredients:
150 grams of margarine
250 grams of caster sugar
150 grams of self-raising flour
125 grams of sour cream
4 medium eggs
50ml of cocoa powder
1 teaspoons of baking powder
2 teaspoons of good quality rosewater

Method:
Preheat the oven to 160ºC (fan assisted) 320ºF/ gas mark 2

Grease and line a ten-inch/26cm rectangle or square loose bottomed baking tin.

Put all the ingredients into a mixer and mix until combined and smooth.

Place the mixture into the tin and bake in the middle of the oven for around 30 minutes or until cracked on top and when a skewer inserted comes out clean.

Leave to cool in the tin for 5 minutes then transfer to a wire cooling rack.

When the cake is cool, decorate it with slivers of pistachio, dried rose petals and a dusting of cocoa powder.

Nooshe jaan!

My Little Persian
Spiced Chocolate Cake

Are we all time poor? When do any of us have time to wonder, ponder, stop and smell the proverbial roses? In fact, the only time that I ever truly stop is when I am cooking, baking or eating. And for the most part these are also rushed events.

But sometimes, on the odd occasion that I do get to enjoy, savour the moment and really take in what I am doing, I want there to be cake involved! Preferably with me eating said cake! But baking it is a mighty fine way to start my downtime!

In my humble opinion, there is not much that feels more indulgent than a yummy slice of chocolate cake! The indulgence, for me, starts the minute the cake goes into the oven.

The smell of a chocolate cake baking is hard to beat. The best kind of pick-me-upper!

This is my ultimate 'go to' recipe when it comes to chocolate cakes. It is so versatile and yummy, and it is a real crowd pleaser. It is light but moist, rich and buttery in texture.

I use this if I am making a cake that requires fondant or buttercream or indeed, just as in this picture, with a dusting of cocoa and some nuts and rose petals.

So, lovely readers, if you can, take some time from your time poor day and eat some cake!

My Little Persian Chocolate Pots

It is a well-known fact that I absolutely love this time of year. All the pretty lights, Christmas music and, of course, all the sweet treats, make everything feel magical.

At this time of year, we tend to have lots of visitors and lots of visitors means oodles of cooking! In our home, no social gathering would be complete without rich and delicious puddings!

This super simple, five-minute dessert is hard to beat in my opinion. It is really easy, and you can get the little ones involved in making it.

My little boy loves mixing it together and watching the cream turn chocolatey and, of course, licking the spoon afterwards! The leftover ganache is also great for making truffles with.

These little pots of heaven have a shiny outer surface and a silky, matt, smooth and rich interior, like all good ganaches should; completely sumptuous!

These super easy chocolate pots are perfect for your Christmas parties and they are real crowd pleasers. If you are stuck for time give them a go and let me know what you think!

You can replace the cardamom with a smidgen of Crème de Menthe if you want a peppermint flavour or some rosewater if you want a Turkish delight treat instead!

Desserts

❦

My Little Persian
Chocolate Pots

Makes around 10 pots
Setting time: 3 -5 hours
Preparation time: 10 minutes

Ingredients:
100 grams of milk chocolate
200 grams of dark chocolate
200ml of double cream
1 teaspoon of ground
cardamom

Method:
Break the chocolate up into chunks in a heat proof bowl.

Pour the cream into a pan and heat slowly until boiling.

Take off the heat and pour over the chocolate, stir until melted.

Add the cardamom and mix until combined.

Pour into small pots and chill for 2 hours before serving. Decorate with sliced almonds and pistachios.

Serve with a biscotti and a glass of ice wine!

Nooshe jaan!

Desserts

❦

Sohan

Makes around 40 sweets
Cooking time: 5-10 minutes
Setting time: 30 minutes

Ingredients:
½ cup of unsalted butter cut into cubes
1 cup of sugar
¼ cup of double cream
¼ cup of maple syrup
2 tablespoons of raw almonds
½ teaspoon of ground saffron dissolved in 1 teaspoon rosewater
2 teaspoons of ground cardamom
½ teaspoon of salt

To Garnish:
2 tablespoons of chopped pistachio
2 tablespoons of barberries (sour cherries) - optional

Method:
Line a baking sheet with baking paper

In a heavy bottomed saucepan, combine the butter, the sugar, the cream, and the maple syrup.

Cook over a medium heat stirring continuously with a wooden spoon.

Bring to a boil (around three to five minutes).

Add the almonds, the saffron, the rosewater, the cardamom and the salt.

Increase the heat and continue cooking without disturbing for around five to ten minutes until the mixture is a deep peanut butter shade of golden brown and the top is getting thicker and bubbling. This last stage is so important as if undercooked it will be elastic and chewy and overcooked it will burn.

Remove from the heat and pour onto a baking tray immediately and cover with the garnish. Allow it to cool completely and then break it into pieces.

Keep refrigerated for around 3 weeks in an airtight container.

Nooshe jaan!

Sohan

When we have guests coming to stay, I always like to have some homemade treats readily available.

Sohan is a favourite childhood sweet of mine. When my dad or my uncle visited home, they would always bring me a few boxes of it and it never lasts longer than a few days in my house. My mouth is watering as I type, which is probably why I will never again be a size eight!

As rose can be quite an acquired taste, I thought that I would attempt to tell a little bit of its story in Persian cooking whilst I wait ever so impatiently for them to set.

Rose is one of the main flavours of Persian cooking, along with turmeric, saffron, pomegranate and cardamom. Pull up a chair at any Iranian restaurant and you'll be sure to find something flavoured with rose on the menu.

The use of rose in Persian cooking dates back as far as the Persian Empire and can be used in both sweet and savoury dishes or indeed just as a beautiful decoration.

It comes in various forms.

Rosewater - is a bi-product of rose oil and is made by steeping the petals in water. Rosewater is most commonly used to infuse flavour into a whole dish, into cake, and into sweets such as gaz, which is a type of nougat, sohan, which is a form of brittle (see the recipe below), or ice-cream.

Dried rose petals - ground into a sugar or into a savoury spice blend such as advieh.

Fresh rose petals - candied for decoration, rosewater jam or, one of my favourites - a rose and cucumber gin and tonic which tastes really clean, crisp and elegant. My uncle told me that my grandmother used to infuse it and drink it in her tea.

Each of the above has a different taste and depth and it never fails to amaze me how versatile one ingredient can be.

However, the story doesn't stop there. For years rose has been used not only in cooking but medicinally, as a top note in some perfumes, to show people that you love them or to just to make them smile.

It is of such importance to Iranians that it is also used to clean for religious ceremonies.

So, if you are one of the lucky people who has received a bunch of beautiful roses, I hope that you have a little smile and that you think about their story.

Desserts

❦

My Little Wimbledon
Noon Khamei

Makes around 10
Cooking time: 30 minutes
Preparation time: 20 minutes

Ingredients:
For the choux pastry:
65 grams of plain flour
Pinch of salt
50 grams of butter
100ml of water
1 teaspoon of sugar
2 medium eggs

Rose flavoured sweet cream:
300 grams of double cream
80 grams of icing sugar
2 teaspoons of rosewater
British strawberries

Method:
Pre-heated the oven to 200ºC fan, 220ºC/425ºF non-fan, gas mark 7.

Place the butter and the sugar into a pan and slowly bring to a boil.

Take off the heat and add all the flour at once and then quickly mix until the batter comes away from the sides of the pan into a ball. Leave to cool for one minute.

Put back on the heat and allow the mixture to emulsify a little (when it sticks to the pan).

Add the eggs (beaten) one at a time, mixing vigorously. It will look slimy at this stage. Make sure that it is thoroughly mixed before you add the second egg and repeat the same process again.

Line a baking sheet with greased baking paper and pipe out small disks, giving each disk enough space to rise.

Place into the pre-heated oven for 25 minutes. Keep an eye on them in the last few minutes, and when they are golden, remove and pierce each one and place them back in the oven for a further five minutes for them to dry out.

Remove and leave to cool on a wire rack then make the cream.

To make the cream, add all ingredients, with the exception of the strawberries, to a bowl and whisk until stiff peaks form.

Add to a piping bag (I use disposable ones as they are so much easier to just throw away afterwards) and pipe into little pastries.

You can dress them with chocolate or leave them plain. I tend to leave them plain as the cream is sweet enough and on this occasion with it being Wimbledon, I added some sliced strawberries.

They were yummy and I ate half the plate!

Nooshe jaan!

My Little Wimbledon Noon Khamei

I spent a day at Wimbledon with my team a few years ago enjoying some lovely company, great tennis and wonderful food!

For as long as I can remember, I have loved watching the amazing chef Michel Roux Jr cooking on television. He is without doubt my favourite chef of all time. He is so graceful and methodical when he cooks, and his public persona is warm and friendly. Well, I had the unbelievable pleasure of seeing him in person while I was at Wimbledon!

Now, ordinarily, I am relatively balanced and sensible and I generally don't get carried away or overly excited. However, this occasion was entirely different! When seeing Michel in person, my power of speech and my ability to smile normally completely evaded me! I was indeed totally awestruck! I've always wondered how I would react if I met him and, well, it's fair to say that I went totally off piste and more than likely, I embarrassed most, if not all my team.

The food at 'The Gatsby Club' was outstanding. In honour of that, and the fact that it's Wimbledon fortnight, I am sincerely hoping to redeem myself with these. I came home inspired to do some fusion cooking and the result is this lovely little strawberry and rose noon khamei. Or strawberry cream puffs if you prefer!

I hope that you enjoy them as much as I do! They are no croquembouche, but they are delightful nonetheless!

Nan-e Keshmeshi

These gorgeous delicate little raisin cookies are lovely with a strong cup of Persian chai and they keep well in the fridge for a few weeks. Be careful though, they are so easy to eat. You could easily consume an entire plateful before you know it! They are also ridiculously easy to make and taste so different from any biscuit or cookie that you would have had before. That reminds me I must make these for my uncle and my aunt the next time they visit!

Desserts

Nan-e Keshmeshi

Makes around 30 cookies
Cooking time: 10 - 15 minutes
Preparation time: 5 minutes

Ingredients:
1 ¼ cup of vegetable oil or melted butter
1 teaspoon of vanilla extract
2 tablespoons of rosewater
Pinch of salt
1 ¼ cup of caster sugar
4 large eggs
1 ¼ cup of raisins or chocolate chips
2 cups of plain flour

Method:
Pre heat oven to 160ºC fan, 175ºC/350ºF non-fan, gas mark 4.

Line a baking sheet with baking paper.

In a large bowl mix together the oil, the vanilla, the rosewater, the salt and the sugar until smooth.

Add the eggs, one at a time, whisking until creamy.

Stir in the raisins or the chocolate chips.

Fold in the flour, using a rubber spatula until a thick batter forms.

Put spoonfuls of the batter onto the baking sheet, leaving two inches between each scoop.

Bake for ten to fifteen minutes until the edges of the cookie are golden brown.

Remove and cool on a wire rack.

When cool, loosen from baking sheet with a metal spatula and store in an airtight container in the fridge until ready to eat.

Nooshe jaan!

Desserts
🌷

Orange Blossom and Cardamom Drizzle Cake

Serves: 10-12
Cooking time: 45-50 minutes
Preparation time: 15 minutes

Ingredients:
225 grams of self-raising flour
75 grams of ground almonds
100 grams of caster sugar
2 medium eggs
250ml of natural yoghurt
150ml of vegetable oil
Zest of 1 orange
1 teaspoon of ground cardamom
1 teaspoon of baking powder

For the drizzle:
100ml of water
100 grams of caster sugar or honey
Juice of 1 Orange
2 teaspoons of good quality orange blossom syrup

To decorate:
Figs, sliced almonds, orange rind
300ml of double cream
½ cup of icing sugar

Method:
I use a 10 inch/26cm loose bottom tin for mine

Preheat oven to 160°C fan, 175°C/350°F non-fan, gas mark 4 and line the baking tin with parchment paper.

Combine the dry ingredients into a mixing bowl and stir.

Mix the eggs, the yoghurt, the honey, the butter, and the zest together and then add to the dry ingredients.

Mix well until combined and place in the tin.

Bake for around 35 to 40 minutes until golden brown and a skewer inserted comes out clean.

Leave to cool in the tin for 15 minutes.

While the cake is cooling poke tiny holes all over the top and make the syrup.

To make the drizzle just add all the ingredients to a pan and bring to a boil then reduce the heat until the mixture has thickened and reduced. This takes about 10 minutes.

When the drizzle is ready, use a spoon and pour over the cake. Leave to settle for a few hours or overnight.

To make the cream, add the icing sugar, the cream and the orange blossom water to a bowl and whisk until stiff peaks form.

Dollop on the cake and spread over the surface and decorate with figs, orange rind, sliced almonds and pistachio slivers.

This is lovely on its own with a coffee or a cup of strong Persian Chai.

Nooshe jaan!

Orange Blossom and Cardamom Drizzle Cake

This lovely little orange blossom and cardamom drizzle cake is amazingly indulgent because not only is it a moist citrus drizzle cake, but it also has a decadent sweet orange blossom cream on top to finish it off.

Be warned though, one slice of this gorgeous little cake is not enough!

This cake is really easy to make. From combining all the dry ingredients, to it being in my belly, took less than one and a half hours in total and that's with cooling time! It takes around five minutes to prepare everything. There are no difficult or technical elements to it at all and it looks very pretty.

I cannot wait to bake this again the next time we have guests over, as I'm sure that it will be a party pleaser!

So, what is orange blossom water? Orange blossom water is a clear liquid with intense, floral-orange aromas. It is made in the same way as rosewater, in that it is made by boiling orange blossom flowers in water, and then capturing and condensing the steam.

Use sparingly, or the flavour can be overpowering. You can purchase them from most good supermarkets in the baking aisle. I got mine from our local Sainsbury's and the brand I use is Cortas.

Cardamom and Orange Blossom Mille-Feuille

On a business trip to Paris I sat outside the Latin quarter with a dear friend of mine.

We listened to a wonderful musician who had such spirit that he found a unique way of bringing his music to the masses. He used a keyboard, a bike and a fish tank.

His music was so mesmerizing that we sought out a coffee shop nearby to listen and to watch.

I had a cup of java and I let the sound wash over me whilst watching people strolling around, stop, talk, kiss, smile and hold hands. It was not the Paris that I went to in December with my husband a few years ago.

That Paris was freezing, dark and beautiful in an entirely different way. This Paris, sitting outside drinking java, felt as if the promise of summer was everywhere.

We moved from one café to another and, in the final one, I enjoyed a glass of Sancerre and a beautiful praline mille-feuille. Every single sense was in delight!

It was crisp, nutty, creamy and immensely satisfying. French cuisine is so revered, with good reason. It made me think about Persian food; my food.

I get inspiration from so many different places and that little café outside the Latin Quarter was one of those places.

Persian cuisine is said to be the oldest in existence and it has given inspiration to so many different cultures and food staples.

This time I'm taking some from Paris and adding a Persian essence to it.

Enter my cardamom and orange blossom mille-feuille!

Desserts

Cardamom and Orange Blossom Mille Feuille

Serves: 4
Cooking time: 25 minutes
Preparation time: 60 minutes

Ingredients:
Shop bought puff pastry (as making your own takes forever and shop bought tastes just as good)
600ml of double cream
1 teaspoon of ground cardamom (I always grind my own as the flavour is stronger)
1 teaspoon of orange blossom extract
A third of a cup of icing sugar
Pistachios to sprinkle

Method:
Preheat the oven to 180ºC fan, 190ºC/375ºF non-fan, gas mark 5.

Cover a baking sheet with a layer of parchment and sprinkle sugar over it.

Lay a sheet of pastry on top and sprinkle with sugar.

Cover with another sheet of parchment and place a heavy baking sheet on top (I also weigh mine down with a large lasagne dish).

Place in the oven for 25 minutes.

Remove and leave on a wire rack to cool.

When cooled, very carefully remove the parchment and slice into matching size rectangles.

When completely cooled make the cream filling.

Add the cream, the icing sugar, the cardamom and the orange blossom to a bowl and whisk until stiff peaks form.

Add to a piping bag (if you want it to look pretty, otherwise just spoon it over) and pipe it onto the first layer of pastry.

Place a sheet of pastry on top and repeat once more.

Sprinkle with icing sugar and decorate.

Enjoy with a strong cup of Persian chai.

Nooshe jaan!

Desserts

Nan-e Panjerehi - Window Cookies

Makes around 30 cookies
Cooking time: 15 - 30
minutes
Preparation time: 20 minutes

Ingredients:
For the Batter:
5 eggs
½ cup of full fat milk
4 teaspoons of rosewater
½ cup of plain flour
½ cup of rice flour
½ cup of cornflour
3 cups of oil for frying

For Dusting:
1 teaspoon of ground
cardamom
1 cup of icing sugar
Dried rose petals to decorate

Method:
Make the dusting first by combining the ingredients in a bowl and set aside.

To make the batter beat the eggs, the rosewater and the milk in a bowl until creamy.

Add the flours and beat well until smooth. It should be the same consistency as pancake batter.

Heat the oil well.

Heat the stamp in the oil first, then dip half of it into the batter.

Plunge the batter coated stamp into the oil and shake gently until the cookie is released into the oil.

When the cookie is cooked (it will be crisp and light golden) remove with a slotted spoon onto some parchment.

Repeat until you have the desired number of cookies.

Leave to cool.

Dust with the dusting mix.

Nooshe jaan!

Nan-e Panjerehi - Window Cookies

My grandmother was a wonderful woman. She had a huge heart and an amazing spirit. She loved to cook, and her cooking was incredible!

To this day, when my dad cooks, he references her cooking and sometimes he will taste something that catches him off guard and you can see it brings back memories of his mum, my mamanie, and he will smile.

She used to come to England when I was a child to visit and, when she did, I used to watch her cook and I would tell her that she was doing it all wrong.

I am sure that she wasn't doing it all wrong, and I am also pretty sure that I was just being a bossy boots, a habit I have retained all these years later; the right of the eldest child!

I guess it is this. These little smiles, the memories and the way that food brings people together, spark a conversation, and evoke a warm feeling inside you, which is yet another reason why I love cooking so much.

These wonderful little Persian pastries are new to me. They have been difficult to master, and they are not for the faint-hearted cook, I warn you.

My aunt gifted me this beautiful kitchen stamp and up until this point I had never tasted or heard of nan-e panjerehi.

There was only one thing for it, I absolutely had to work out how to use it. It was a gift to her from my mamanie and now to me. If you find yourself with one of these and you can find the time to make these cookies, you must try them!

They are beautiful and they taste so delicate that it is really hard to describe.

Some tips before you start.

Get the oil really hot and dip the stamp in the oil before dipping it into the batter. This ensures that the batter slips off into the oil easily when dipped.

Only half dip the stamp in the batter, otherwise you end up with the whole stamp covered and the cookie won't come off.

Desserts

Persian Sesame Brittle
(Sohan Asali)

Makes around 2 kilner jars full
Cooking time: 10 minutes
Preparation time: 5 minutes

Ingredients:
½ cup of granulated sugar
3 tablespoons of runny honey
1 dessert spoon of rosewater
¾ cup of sesame seeds
¼ teaspoon of ground cinnamon
pinch of nutmeg

Method:
Place some baking paper onto a baking sheet and set aside.

Melt the sugar, the honey and the rosewater in a pan over a moderate heat for around five minutes until combined.

Add the remaining ingredients and stir.

Cook for around 20 minutes stirring occasionally until the mixture turns to a nice golden colour.

Pour out onto the baking sheet and leave to cool.

Once cool, snap into pieces and store in an airtight jar or container for around a month.

Nooshe jaan!

Persian Sesame Brittle (Sohan Asali)

To celebrate my little sister turning thirty, we did something that we haven't done in years. We escaped for a few hours to spend some time together and just natter about everything and nothing in particular. It was absolutely lovely.

We see so little of each other nowadays, partly because we live at opposite ends of the country and partly because we both like to fill our every spare moment planning things to do and adventures to take our little boys on. Before you know it, the year has gone by and then we are planning our annual Christmas get together!

We talked about how 'time poor' everyone is and how no one ever really stops nowadays. She spoke about her job and her boys and her upcoming house move and I rambled on about my boys, my blog, work and food. Then invariably, the conversation would move on to memories of us being younger and more carefree and the endless tricks that we would play on each other, which we continued into our early adult years.

One occasion in particular that she reminded me of, then promptly told me that I had to write a blog about when she stopped laughing, was the first Christmas that I decided to make homemade sweets for all of our close family and friends.

I made an enormous amount of peanut brittle and I placed it in little glass jars tied with raffia and I labelled them all. It's something that my husband and I have continued to do every year, although the initial jar of sweets has now somewhat grown into a production line of jams, sauces, chutney and flavoured gin!

My sister ate an entire jar of my peanut brittle and then she hounded me for the recipe. At this point I was feeling quite mischievous (it was probably the wine) so I said, "Okay, you do this ..."

I told her the recipe step by step and then I told her to let the sugar boil until it went a really dark mahogany. I said, and I quote, and I will never live this down to this day ...

"Don't you worry if it goes black. Don't touch it. It will lighten when you add the peanut; something to do with the salt and a chemical reaction! Let it go black, as black as my scarf and keep cooking!" Oh dear. Well. She did it.

She then phoned me to give me a right good telling off because she did exactly as I said and had completely burned one of her Circulon pans beyond repair. It was really mean but happily, we (I) still laugh about it to this day. She did tell me, however, that she will never make one of my recipes again unless I publish it on my blog.

So, in honour of my lovely little sister's burnt pan, here is my Persian sesame brittle, which is hugely popular in Iran and I absolutely love it. I find it a lot easier to eat than peanut brittle and it has a nice crunch to it too. Try it out and let me know what you think, and I promise you, you won't burn your pans in the process! I warn you though, it is incredibly moreish!

This one is for Gaby, my lovely and very patient little sister. xx

Desserts

❧

Persian Almond and Pistachio Baklava

Makes around 30 pieces
Cooking time: 25-30 minutes
Preparation time: 20 minutes

Ingredients:
6 sheets of filo pastry
75 grams of sliced pistachios
120 grams of ground almonds
50 grams of caster sugar
Grated rind of half a large orange
Grated rind of 1 lime
1 teaspoon of ground cardamom
½ teaspoon of cinnamon
80 grams of melted butter
Dried rose petals and ground pistachios to garnish

Orange Blossom Syrup:
100ml of water
1 teaspoon of freshly squeezed lime juice
1 teaspoon of orange blossom water
150 grams of caster sugar
1 clove

Method:
Preheat the oven to 160°C fan, 175°C/350°F non-fan, gas mark 4.

Combine the nuts, the sugar, the spices and the rind in a bowl and set aside.

Butter a baking dish and layer with three sheets of filo pastry making sure that you butter each sheet before placing the other on top.

Add the filling all at once to the dish and place a sheet of filo pastry on top.

Place another two layers of filo pastry on top making sure that you butter each sheet individually before placing the next.

Lightly butter the top sheet and score into squares with a sharp knife.

Place in a pre-heated oven for 20 minutes until golden.

While this is cooking start to make the syrup.

Add all the ingredients to a pan and simmer gently for around 20 minutes until the syrup thickens.

Pour the syrup over the baklava as soon as you remove it from the oven and leave it to cool completely before removing it from the tin.

Nooshe jaan!

Persian Almond and Pistachio Baklava

Baklava is sweet, sticky and flaky at the same time. It is the ultimate overindulgence and it is generally made using filo pastry, butter, nuts, syrup or honey.

It is thought to originate in Turkey where trays of it were presented during ceremonies.

It is an alternative to a dessert, and it is usually served with a cup of strong Persian chai, especially around the festival of Nowruz (Iranian New Year and the start of spring).

I myself absolutely love it at any time of the year with afternoon tea.

This is a recipe for Persian baklava. There are many different variations to baklava depending on the country that you are in.

However, traditionally Persian baklava comprises almonds and pistachios with a sweet orange blossom syrup instead of the heavy honey-based syrup commonly used in Turkish and Greek baklava.

It is my favourite of all the different variations.

Sholeh Zard

Sholeh zard is a delicious Persian saffron rice pudding. The name literally means yellow (zard) fire (sholeh).

These little bowls of sunshine bring joy to everyone who eats them. Traditionally, this dessert is served to symbolise the pledge you make at weddings or at funerals, or at the feast of Nazri where food is given to the poor.

It is my absolute all-time favourite sweet and as a treat, if I was feeling poorly or for my birthday, my dad used to make it for me. It takes a few hours, but the end result is wonderful, and it is reasonably cheap to make if your pantry is stocked with spices.

Just one cup of rice makes so much that you could make it for a dinner party and still have leftovers to enjoy for the next few days.

I used to love eating it straight from the fridge, ice cold with just a sprinkling of cinnamon and I still do. It's my ultimate secret indulgence.

From my table to yours. I hope that you make it and enjoy it as much as I do.

Desserts

Sholeh Zard

Serves: 8
Cooking time: 80 minutes
Preparation time: 10 minutes

Ingredients:
1 cup of basmati rice
6 cups of water
3 cups of sugar
1/3 cup of rosewater
1/2 teaspoon of saffron
threads

Method:
Wash the rice until it runs clear. This gets rid of the starch.

Add the rice to a good sized strong bottomed pan with the water. Bring to a boil and skim off the rising foam.

Turn down the heat and simmer for an hour with the lid on, occasionally stirring, to make sure that it doesn't stick to the bottom of the pan.

Add the sugar and the saffron liquid and cook for a further 20 minutes.

By this point the rice should be soft with barely any liquid left. If not, cook for a little longer. When the top becomes creamy it is done!

Add the rosewater just before you remove it from the heat.

Spoon into bowls and cool in the fridge.

When cool, decorate with cinnamon powder and pistachio slivers. Enjoy!

Nooshe jaan!

Desserts

Raspberry and Rose Madeleines

Makes: 12
Cooking time: 10 minutes
Preparation time: 20 minutes

Ingredients:
2 medium-sized free-range eggs
½ teaspoon of rosewater
1 teaspoon of lime zest
125 grams of icing sugar
100 grams of plain flour - sifted
¼ teaspoon of baking powder - sifted
125 grams of melted baking fat or butter
10 grams of dried raspberry pieces

Method:
Pre-heat the oven to 180ºC fan, 190ºC/400ºF non-fan, gas mark 6.

Grease and flour a madeline pan. Mine is a 12-mould pan and I use it twice.

To a mixing bowl add the eggs, the rosewater and the lime and whisk for 5 minutes until thick and creamy.

Add the icing sugar and continue to whisk for a further 2 minutes.

Add half the flour and the baking powder and gently fold into the egg mixture.

Fold in the left-over flour and the baking powder and the dried raspberry.

Fold in the cooled melted butter and spoon it into the moulds until each one is filled.

Bake for 10 minutes or until golden and the sponge springs back when touched.

Loosen with a knife and serve straight away.

Nooshe jaan!

Raspberry and Rose Madeleines

The weekend started like this...

Me: "Kasper, you could help mummy make some cakes this morning if you like?"

Kasper: "Hmmm I could, but I'm not gonna!"

I stopped dead in my tracks wondering when my little baby boy turned into a little man with a very strong mind of his own.

I decided to make some madeleines, in a bid to get him to help me anyway. It worked.

As soon as my Smeg mixer started whirring, his ears pricked up and he spun round to ask, "Mummy, can I help please."

Phew! Normality restored ... for now anyway! And where on earth did he learn the word "gonna"!

These dense little cakes are the perfect start to a lazy Saturday with a strong black coffee.

I have adapted the classic French recipe and I added some lovely fresh Persian flavours.

Chocolate and Pistachio Cupcakes

Easter has arrived and what better way to spend it than eating chocolate cake with family.

These little chocolate and pistachio cupcakes won't disappoint.

I have used a pistachio essence in the frosting to give a real pistachio flavour, rather than just a green vanilla butter icing.

Some recipes will tell you to use a pistachio pudding mix to give you the flavour. It's entirely up to you.

However, I prefer a real homemade butter icing for my cupcakes. I bought the essence I use online and it works well.

The key to really lovely cupcakes is to make the cake batter really light, and they should be served chilled as, let's face it, it's all about the buttercream with these little gems and no one wants a warm buttercream!

I normally use cacao powder in my chocolate cupcakes but as it's Easter I have used real melted chocolate in these and they are yummy!

Desserts

Chocolate and Pistachio Cupcakes

Makes: 24 mini cupcakes
Cooking time: 15 minutes
Preparation time: 20 minutes

Ingredients:
115 grams of 'Green & Blacks' dark chocolate
85 grams of margarine - room temperature
175 grams of soft brown sugar
2 large free-range eggs - room temperature
185 grams of plain flour - sifted
¾ teaspoon of baking powder
¾ teaspoon of bicarbonate of soda
250ml of full fat milk
1 teaspoon of Madagascan vanilla essence

For the Frosting:
250 grams of unsalted butter
500 grams of icing sugar
1 tablespoon of full fat milk
1 teaspoon of pistachio essence
1 teaspoon of green food colouring
Pistachio slivers to decorate

Method:
Preheat the oven to 170ºC fan, 180ºC/350ºF non-fan, gas mark 4.

Line a cupcake tray with paper cupcake cases.

Melt the chocolate in the microwave for 30 seconds stir and blast for another 30 seconds. Be careful not to burn it. Leave to cool.

In a mixing bowl, cream the butter and the sugar until pale and smooth.

In a separate bowl, whisk the eggs until thick and creamy.

Add the melted chocolate to the eggs and mix gently.

Add the egg mixture to the butter and the sugar and beat well.

Combine the flour, the bicarbonate of soda and the baking powder in a separate bowl.

Add the milk to a milk jug with the vanilla.

Pour half the milk and the flour into the chocolate mixture and mix well until combined.

Repeat with the remaining flour and milk.

Do not beat as you will remove all the air from the mixture if you do and you will end up with little chocolate pancakes instead of cupcakes!

Carefully spoon the mixture into the cupcake cases. This is a very liquid batter so you can pour in if you prefer. Fill to two thirds full.

If making mini cupcakes like I have, bake for 15 minutes until a skewer inserted comes out clean.

Or if making large cupcakes bake for 20-25 minutes.

Remove from the oven and leave them to cool while you make the frosting.

To make the frosting, put all the ingredients into a large food processor and blitz.

Pipe onto cooled cupcakes.

Decorate with pistachio slivers and set in the fridge for an hour before eating.

Nooshe jaan!

Desserts

Yazdi Cupcakes

Makes 24 cupcakes
Cooking time: 20 minutes
Preparation time: 5 minutes

Ingredients:
1 cup of vegetable oil
1 ½ cups of light brown sugar
Juice of 1 lime
1 tablespoon of rosewater
4 eggs separated
1 cup of full fat plain yoghurt
1 teaspoon of bicarbonate of soda
1 teaspoon of baking powder
¼ teaspoon of salt
1 tablespoon of ground cardamom
2 cups of plain flour

Method:
Pre-heat the oven to 160ºC fan, 175ºC/350ºF non-fan, gas mark 4.

Line 2 muffin tins with cupcake wrappers (makes around 30).

Mix together the oil, the sugar, the lime and the rosewater.

Slowly add the egg yolks one at a time to the mixture.

Add the yoghurt and mix until creamy.

Mix all the dry ingredients together and then add to the wet mixture. Mix for a minute but do not over mix as this will make them chewy and not light.

Mix the egg whites until stiff peaks form, then gently fold into the cake mixture.

Bake for around 20 minutes or until a tester comes out clean. I added a few ground pistachios and rose petals to the batter before baking.

Cool on a wire rack.

Try not to eat them all at once!

Nooshe jaan!

Yazdi Cupcakes

Cardamom is one of my favourite spices to use in Persian cooking in both sweet and savoury dishes. It is the third most expensive spice by weight in the world behind vanilla and saffron and, just like these two, it is divine.

I always keep a jar of both ground cardamom and cardamom pods in my pantry as they have such different uses.

I do prefer to grind my own cardamom as it's a lot fresher that way and I tend to find that the ground cardamom that you buy in the supermarkets loses much of its flavour as soon as it is opened.

The flavour evaporates once the pods are ground and the process lowers the flavour and the value of these little seeds.

If a recipe asks for one and a half teaspoons of ground cardamom, I would recommend using around ten pods.

If, like me, you decide to mill your own, make sure that you remove the husks first! So many people I know grind the whole lot and the husk has less flavour and a nasty chewy texture. Some people use it like chewing gum, although goodness knows why!

It's the glorious little black seeds inside the husks that you want, so forget the rest! It's also quite therapeutic de-shelling them!

Green cardamom has a slightly resinous and aromatic flavour and I find that it is better suited to sweet dishes than black cardamom.

Black cardamom is great to use if you want to add a touch of smokiness and a coolness similar to mint to a dish.

These little traditional Persian yazdi cupcakes use green cardamom and are one of my favourites to make. They are quite technical but are worth the effort.

I sometimes ice them with a pistachio buttercream which makes them look and taste even more beautiful, but this time I left them plain, with a simple scattering of pistachios and rose petals on the raw batter.

If you do make them, I hope that you love them as much as I do.

Desserts

❦

Chocolate and Pistachio Truffles

Makes around 40 truffles
Cooking time: 2 minutes
Preparation time: 20 minutes
and 3 hours setting time

Ingredients:
300 grams of dark chocolate
300 ml of double cream
50 grams of butter
½ cup of pistachios
1 teaspoon of ground cardamom

Method:
Chop the chocolate and place it into a mixing bowl.

Put the cream and the butter into a pan and heat until gently simmering.

When heated pour the cream over the chocolate and stir until the chocolate has melted.

Chop the pistachios and add to the chocolate mixture, along with the ground cardamom.

Refrigerate for two to three hours.

Remove from the fridge when set.

Using a teaspoon, scoop some of the mixture into your hands and roll it into a small ball.

Dip in cacao mixed with a little ground cardamom to take the bitterness away.

Eat as quickly as you can and deny all knowledge of their existence so that you don't have to share! Or give as a gift to have after a lovely meal.

Nooshe jaan!

Chocolate and Pistachio Truffles

My husband and I are both runners. Have I mentioned this before? Maybe not. Well, he likes to run in the evening, and I like to run in the morning, as by seven p.m. it is a lesser known fact that I turn into a sloth and I cannot condone any exercise at all. I prefer to use this time to eat really good food or chocolate! Judge me if you will. I judge me. I still do it.

Whilst my husband is out running, I frantically search the house for some truffles. I cannot for the life of me find any (he must have hidden them all) so I decide to make some myself in the hope that they will be rolled, dipped in cacao and in my mouth whilst watching an American TV show (my other addiction) before he steps foot in the door later and when he asks, "What have you done this evening?" I can casually say, "Oh, I ate an apple, did some really important spreadsheet work of some description and did not eat any homemade truffles AT ALL."

He will instantly know that I am lying my bum off by the smell of melted chocolate wafting through the house.

That and the fact that I have cacao on my nose as I type.

Oh well. He married me knowing about my chocolate addiction (oh and my hundreds of pairs of shoes!).

If you are a chocolate truffle fan like me, I urge you to give these a try.

Desserts

✿

Almond and Lime, Rosewater Drizzle Cake

Serves: 12
Cooking time: 45 - 50 minutes
Preparation time: 20 minutes

Ingredients:
225 grams of self-raising flour
75 grams of ground almonds
100 grams of coconut sugar
2 medium eggs
250ml of natural yoghurt
150ml of melted butter or vegetable oil (I use oil in mine)
2 tablespoons of runny honey
Zest of 2 limes
1 teaspoon of baking powder

For the Drizzle:
100ml of water
100 grams of caster sugar
3 tablespoons of runny honey
2 teaspoons of good quality rosewater

To Decorate:
Sliced pistachios and edible rose petals
I use a fluted 10-inch loose bottom tin for my Almond and Lime, Rosewater Drizzle Cake

Method:
Preheat the oven to 160ºC fan 320ºF/ gas mark 2.

Line the baking tin with parchment paper.

Combine the dry ingredients into a mixing bowl and stir.

Add the lime zest to the dry ingredients and mix for 2 minutes. This breaks the oils down in the zest and helps the flavour infuse the batter.

Mix the eggs, the yoghurt, the honey and the butter together and then add to the dry ingredients.

Mix well until combined and place in the baking tin.

Bake for around 45 to 50 minutes until golden brown and a skewer comes out clean.

Leave to cool in the tin for 15 minutes.

While the cake is cooling, poke tiny holes all over the top and make the drizzle.

To make the drizzle, just add all the ingredients to a pan and bring to a boil, then reduce the heat until the mixture has thickened and has reduced. This takes about 10 minutes.

When the drizzle is ready, use a spoon and pour it over the cake.

Leave to settle for a few hours or overnight then slice and decorate.

This is lovely on its own with a coffee or a cup of strong Persian Chai or as a dessert with a rosewater cream.

Nooshe jaan!

Almond and Lime, Rosewater Drizzle Cake

Whilst having a bit of a spring clean, I got distracted (as I normally do) by my countless recipe books, some of which I haven't opened in forever. So instead of carrying on with my spring cleaning and eating the proverbial frog on the plate, I did what all great procrastinators do and I grabbed a coffee and I sat down to read and I lost about two hours poring over recipes and meals that I haven't eaten in years.

One of the books that I came across was St Michael, Sweet Temptation. It was a cookery book produced by M&S. If you have never heard of this book, I am not entirely surprised as it's older than I am. However, if you ever come across one in a charity shop, it is a must buy. Snatch it from whoever is about to purchase it and spend the potential 50p (I think that is the going rate for a book in a charity shop nowadays?) and take it home and cherish it forever. You will be glad that you did!

This book was passed down to me by my mum when I bought my first house and I will always remember making my first ever batch of profiteroles myself and they didn't rise at all, not even a smidge. In-fact I burnt the lot and had to throw them away.

However, this is a book I that I will always go back to when I want a classic pastry recipe and it hasn't failed me since the disastrous little black disks that were desperate to call themselves profiteroles but never made the cut!

I'll leave you with this yummy version of almond and lime, rosewater drizzle cake. I found the recipe scribbled on a piece of paper and I later used it as a bookmark in this book. Thank heavens for procrastination!

My Little Persian Mille Feuille

A few years ago, my husband made me a beautiful Persian love cake for my birthday. It was a delicate cardamom chiffon sponge, with a delicious fresh cream filling, flavoured with rosewater with candied rose petals and pistachios. It was incredible.

I am unashamed to say that I ate pretty much the entire cake, bar one slice that he had, and I loved every mouthful. As legend would have it, the Persian love cake was originally made by a Persian woman who was madly in love with a prince. To make him fall in love with her, she baked him this cake and she filled it with magical love powers.

Now, as beautiful as the cake is, there are two endings to the legend. The first and most popular ending is that the prince returned her love and that they lived happily ever after. In the second he doesn't and, even more heart-breaking, we don't find out what happened to the cake!

My favourite ending is the first! I mean, who wouldn't fall in love with someone who made them a beautiful love cake? Or any cake for that matter! Just the name evokes a sense of opulence, indulgence and romance. All good things in a cake, don't you think?

So, in honour of this enchanting cake, I have created a pastry version that has the same flavours and key spices running through it. For all of you love birds out there ... or indeed anyone who loves cake as much as I do ... here's one for you!

Desserts

My Little Persian Mille Feuille Recipe

Serves: 4
Cooking time: 25 minutes
Preparation time: 20 minutes

Ingredients:
Shop bought puff pastry
(as making your own takes
forever and shop bought stuff
tastes just as good)
600 ml of double cream
1 teaspoon of rose water
Third of a cup icing sugar

For the Syrup:
150 grams of caster sugar
100ml of water
1 teaspoon of rosewater
Pistachios to sprinkle

Method:
Preheat the oven to 180°C fan, 190°C/375°F non-fan, gas mark 5.

Cover a baking sheet with a layer of parchment and sprinkle sugar over it.

Lay a sheet of pastry on top and sprinkle with sugar

Cover with another sheet of parchment and place heavy baking sheet on top. (I also weigh mine down with a large lasagne dish).

Place in the oven for 25 minutes.

Remove and leave on a wire rack to cool.

When cooled very carefully remove the parchment and slice into matching size rectangles.

While cooling make the rose sugar syrup.

Add the water, the rosewater and the sugar to a pan and bring to a boil.

Reduce the heat and simmer until thickened.

When thickened, spoon over the cut pastry slices and leave to set.

When completely cooled, and set, make the cream filling.

Add the cream, the icing sugar and the rose to a bowl and whisk until stiff peaks form.

Add to a piping bag (if you want it to look pretty, otherwise just spoon it over) and pipe it onto the first layer of pastry.

Place a sheet of pastry on top and repeat once more.

Sprinkle with icing sugar and decorate.

Enjoy with a strong cup of Persian Chai.

Nooshe jaan!

Desserts

❦

Noon Khamei
(Sweet Rose Profiteroles)

Makes: 12
Cooking time: 30- 40 minutes
Preparation time: 10 minutes

Ingredients:
For the choux pastry:
65 grams of plain flour
Pinch of salt
50 grams of butter
100ml of water
1 teaspoon of sugar
2 medium eggs

**For the Rose flavoured
sweet cream:**
300 grams of double cream
80 grams of icing sugar
2 teaspoons of rosewater

Method:
Preheat the oven to 180ºC fan, 190ºC/375ºF non-fan, gas mark 5.

Place the butter, the sugar and the water into a pan and bring it to a boil slowly.

Take it off the heat.

Add all the flour at once and quickly mix until the batter comes away from the sides of the pan into a ball.

Leave to cool for five minutes.

Add the eggs one at a time mixing vigorously. It will look slimy at this stage. Make sure that it is thoroughly mixed before you add the second egg and repeat the same again.

Line a baking sheet with greased baking paper and pipe out small disks, giving each disk enough space to rise.

Place into the pre-heated oven for 40 minutes. Keep an eye on them at the last few minutes and when they are golden, remove and pierce each one and place them back into the oven for a further five minutes for them to dry out.

Remove and leave to cool on a wire rack then make the cream.

• To make the cream, add all the ingredients to a bowl and whisk until stiff peaks form. Add to a piping bag (I use disposable ones as they are so much easier to just throw away afterwards) and pipe into the pastries.

• You can dress them with chocolate, or you can leave them plain. I tend to leave them plain as the cream is sweet enough and that is how they are traditionally served in Iran. However, feel free to add chocolate if you are going for the ultimate indulgence and trust me these are worth it!

Nooshe jaan!

Noon Khamei
(Sweet Rose Profiteroles)

When my little boy and I make some noon khamei together, it always brings back some lovely memories of summer holidays spent staying with my aunt and my uncle in Suffolk. My aunt and I used to go and meet my uncle for lunch and take him some sandwiches (tuna on brown bread with pickle!).

She used to say, "Tough as old boots that bread!" which always made me giggle and wonder what old boots tasted like! Thankfully I have never found out, despite some epic cooking failures over the years!

On one occasion, we made some choux pastry together. It was a warm summer that year and I remember us making these in the morning and then heading out for the day. I can't remember exactly why, but my uncle had, by the time we arrived back, covered the choux pastry that my aunt had left out to settle, with a damp cloth which obviously ruined them and we didn't get to have lovely little sweet cream pastries that evening!

Anyway, in the twenty-six or so years since that event, my aunt has shown me how to make a good choux pastry batter and this one almost never fails! I have added a few different flavours to the cream, however.

Feel free to adapt to any flavour combination that you like. Cardamom is also a flavour that works well with these.

Happy baking!

My Little Persian Carrot Cake

So, it is no great secret that I love to bake and eat cakes. One of my favourite cakes to bake is this moist, light and surprisingly healthy (I say surprisingly as I make it) spiced carrot cake. These started off as carrot muffins when I was weaning our little one. He absolutely loved devouring and squishing these. They had no flour and no sugar, so they were super healthy and packed full of vegetables. They then developed into something a little less healthy and a little naughtier ... although they are still way less naughty than an ordinary carrot cake!

Desserts

My Little Persian Carrot Cake Recipe

Makes: 12 slices
Cooking time: 45- 60 minutes
Preparation time: 10 minutes

Ingredients:
3 large free-range eggs
100 grams of coconut sugar
1 teaspoon of vanilla extract
100 grams of ground almonds
100 grams of plain flour
100 grams of desiccated coconut
2 teaspoon of ground cinnamon
150 grams of vegetable oil
3 large carrots grated
100 grams of shelled pistachio nuts

Method:
Preheat oven to 140ºC fan, 150ºC/300ºF non-fan, gas mark 2.

Line a ten inch/26cm square loose bottomed cake tin with parchment to cover the bottom and the sides.

Beat the eggs, the sugar and the vanilla.

Add the ground almonds, the plain flour, the coconut and the spices and stir.

Add in the grated carrots and nuts and stir.

Finally, add the vegetable oil and mix until combined. This is a really stiff mixture so don't be tempted to add any additional liquid to the mix.

Pour into the cake tin and place in the centre of the oven.

Cook for around 35 to 40 minutes until risen and firm to the touch.

Leave to cool in the tin.

Serve these with a flavoured cream.

Nooshe jaan!

My Little Persian
Chocolate and Pistachio Torte

I read somewhere that January is the most depressing month of the year and that most people spend it giving up all the things that they love! Well, is there any wonder that it's depressing? I for one can never do that. I rarely make New Year's resolutions, however, if I do, they are generally about doing more of the things that I/we have loved doing throughout the year that we are about to close off.

We have a tradition of filling a jar with little notes throughout the year as a family; about all the things that we have done or have experienced that have made us smile. We then read them all on New Year's Day, and we talk about all the things that we are thankful for and that we want to do more of in the coming year. So, in the spirit of not giving up the things that you love ... here is a scrummy recipe for a super-rich and indulgent chocolate torte! Is it just me or does everything feel a little bit better with chocolate?

Believe it or not, I don't have a particularly sweet tooth.

I have never been one for those sugary jelly sweets or hard-boiled ones, or overly sweet cakes with oodles of icing sugar, but, I have always had a penchant for chocolate. Chocolate of any kind, I'm not fussy. Although, I must confess that my absolute favourite secret indulgence is Cadbury's Whole Nut! Oh, and those yummy praline Belgium chocolate shells. In fact, any chocolate, with any nut in it! I ate two hundred and fifty grams of whole nut a day when I was pregnant with my little boy and to my sheer amazement, I had put on five stone!

Yes, I did say five stone! I wish that I was exaggerating! I couldn't believe it! I was baffled and I put it down to two things:

1. Water retention
2. A big baby

Clearly, I was delusional. It could not possibly have been the sheer volume of sugar that I was consuming. During the day and during the night, I would wake up craving sugar and rustle around the bedside cabinet until I came across a packet of chocolate buttons and ate them out of the palm of my hand, which, my husband said was like sleeping next to a noisy hamster!

It's nearly four years on and countless runs later and thankfully all the weight has gone. However, if I so much as sniff a bar of whole nut, it is gone before my husband can silently scream, "Noo, step away from the sugar and saturated fat." I can't help myself.

You see, the combination of hazelnuts and chocolate or any nuts and chocolate for that matter is divine. Nothing else comes close to it. So, in an ode to my nutty, chocolatey, chocolate nut addiction, I have adapted a recipe that I found online, on Pinterest I think, for a chocolate torte, and I've added some additional elements to it. It literally could not be any easier than this! It is the ultimate quick chocolate fix, but it is also a huge crowd pleaser if you need a quick dessert for a dinner party. If you have the same love of the ultimate duo as me, you need to give this a go! And if you do, please send me a photo or tag me on Instagram before you eat it all, so I can share the chocolatey joy!

Desserts

❦

My Little Persian
Chocolate and Pistachio Torte

Serves: 10
Preparation time: 20 minutes
Setting time: 3 hours

Ingredients:
100 grams of dark chocolate
200 grams of milk chocolate
3 packs of double chocolate
cookies such as bourbons
110 grams of butter melted
200ml of double cream
1 teaspoon of cardamom
50 grams of sliced pistachios
Cocoa powder to dust

Method:
Add the cookies to a food processor and blitz until fine.

Mix the melted butter with the cookies and press into a loose bottomed tin. I use a rectangular one; however, you can use round also.

Put it into the fridge to chill and set while you make the ganache.

To make the ganache, break up the chocolate and put it into a bowl.

Heat the cream gently and pour over the chocolate

Stir until all is melted.

Add a handful of pistachios and the cardamom.

Mix well and pour over the base.

Sprinkle with the remaining pistachios and leave to set for a few hours before serving.

Nooshe jaan!

Thank you for reading and I hope you enjoy cooking and baking these recipes as much as I loved creating them. Befar'ma'id. Khaleymamnoonam.

Rebekah x

Index

A

B

C

D

E

F

Fennel 24
Fig 174
Flatbread 26, 35, 36, 45, 54, 71, 73, 85, 95

G

Garlic 24, 29, 35, 39, 46, 48, 52, 55, 57, 58, 60, 62, 65, 71, 73, 76, 81, 84, 87, 89,
     90, 92, 97, 104, 109, 112, 115, 122, 131, 132, 134, 135, 136
Gherkins 45
Ginger 24, 104

H

Hummus 57

K

Kebab 15, 46, 48, 88, 97, 98, 100, 102, 103
Kuku 26, 37, 39

L

Lamb 22, 40, 41, 42, 76, 78, 83, 84, 88, 92, 94, 100, 102, 103, 109, 110, 115, 121,
     122, 123, 132, 136
Lemon 24, 55, 57, 81, 89, 90, 104, 105, 112, 115, 143

M

Meatballs 133, 134, 135
Mint 30, 68, 84, 92

O

Olives 104
Onion 19, 35, 39, 40, 45, 51, 68, 76, 81, 84, 85, 87, 92, 97, 100, 104, 109, 112,
     115, 118, 122, 134, 135, 136
Orange 76, 152, 188
Orange Blossom 151, 152, 155, 157, 174, 175, 176, 177, 178, 188, 190

P

Parsley 21, 39, 109
Pastry 40, 41, 42, 168, 178, 179, 188, 190, 208, 209, 210, 211, 212, 214
Peas 45, 112
Pepper 24, 35, 39, 45, 51, 55, 57, 68, 76, 81, 97, 100, 109, 115, 118, 122, 135,
     136, 139
Pesto 52, 54

Pine nuts 57, 92
Pistachio 54, 81, 105, 126, 135, 158, 164, 175, 193, 197, 198, 199, 203, 217
Pomegranate 76, 81, 84, 85, 92, 105, 118, 122, 123, 166
Potato 43, 45, 52, 54, 58, 60, 61, 87, 88, 111, 112, 121, 122, 137, 139
Prawns 89, 90

R

raisins 29, 94, 173
Rice 11, 15, 20, 21, 26, 27, 29, 48, 65, 66, 76, 78, 79, 81, 82, 88, 100, 111, 112,
        116, 118, 122, 125, 126, 127, 128, 129, 131, 132, 133, 134, 135, 136, 137,
        139, 145, 156, 181, 191, 193
Rosewater 19, 20, 76, 97, 115, 158, 161, 164, 166, 167, 168, 173, 176, 181, 184,
        193, 194, 201, 206, 207, 208, 209, 210, 212

S

Sabzi 15, 21, 26, 37, 39, 67, 103, 109, 110, 116
Saffron 20, 24, 26, 76, 87, 88, 97, 99, 104, 112, 115, 118, 122, 133, 134, 136, 164,
        166, 191, 193, 202
Salt 21, 28, 29, 35, 39, 45, 51, 58, 62, 68, 76, 81, 84, 87, 97, 100, 109, 115, 118,
        121, 122, 123, 126, 131, 134, 135, 136, 137, 164, 168, 173, 187, 201, 212
Shortbread 147, 148
Soup 25, 26, 29, 30, 60, 61, 62, 73, 111, 121
Split Peas 112
Spring Onions 39, 45, 84, 85
Stew 110, 111, 112, 115, 116, 118, 120, 123
Strawberry 170
Sumac 35, 40, 42, 68, 89, 90, 100
Sweet Potato 49, 51

T

Tadig 112, 126, 139
Tagine 73, 81, 104, 106, 110, 122
Tarragon 45
Tomato 20, 43, 45, 60, 68, 100, 112, 115, 122, 136

W

Walnuts 30, 48

Y

Yoghurt 27, 29, 30, 36, 37, 45, 71, 84, 89, 92, 93, 97, 133, 134, 152, 155, 157,
        174, 201, 206

CPSIA information can be obtained
at www.ICGtesting.com
Printed in the USA
BVHW011418230722
642857BV00007B/383